Putting
My Mind
and Heart
to *Educational Equity*

Memoirs of an Advocate

By Peter D. Roos

CAL
CENTER FOR APPLIED LINGUISTICS

Other Books from the Center for Applied Linguistics:

- A History of Applied Linguistics: From 1980s to the Present
- Adult Biliteracy in the United States
- Adult English Proficiency Assessments
- American Bilingual Tradition
- America's Languages: Investing in Language Education for the 21st Century
- An Insider's Guide to SIOP Coaching
- Ask a Test Developer—A CAL Commentary
- Assessment for Language Instructors: The Basics—Online Course
- BEST Literacy Test Manual
- Bilingualism in Schools and Society

Project editor: M. Beatriz Arias, Ph.D., CAL senior research scientist

Cover art: "Schooling for All," 2015, by Christian Faltis, used courtesy of the artist

www.cal.org

ISBN: 978-1-64669-551-5

Library of Congress Control Number: 2020901517

Recommended citation:
Roos, P. D. (2020). *Putting my mind and heart to educational equity: Memoirs of an advocate.* Washington, DC: Center for Applied Linguistics.

Printed in the United States of America

Contents

Foreword

Education policy is composed of complex relationships between politics, laws, practice, and theories of teaching and student learning. While most education is enacted locally, branches of government at both state and federal levels are involved. And because education is a public enterprise, the stakeholders are many—played out in the environment of locally elected school boards, administrators, teachers' unions, and advocacy organizations. Where do the voices and equal rights of marginalized communities fit into this busy picture?

As a civil rights lawyer, Peter Roos has been something of an artist, painting on this canvas with the lawyerly instruments available to him, getting involved in key interpretations of the equal protection clauses of the Constitution and civil rights laws, especially in how meaningful access is granted through instruction in a language that students can understand. But with the sensitivity of an artist, he has worked the complex environment with an understanding of the power and limitations of his tools combined with a fine sense of whom to push, when, and how.

Roos's awareness of the context and attention to nuance constitute the basis of his effectiveness, and the lessons he shares will benefit those in every field, not just law or education. His heart and intellect together helped him to understand the perspective of the court, the defendant, and the broader society in order to win justice for the underserved. The book at times overflows with his joy for the work and reveals Roos's ample gusto for life. His life has been an adventure full of love for his wife, Emma, and for his many close colleagues, particularly Roger Rice (of

Rice/Roos and Roos/Rice fame). Roos is living proof of the difference that one person can make within this complex world. This memoir shows us how he did it.

To list a few important court cases in which Roos has been involved:

- *United States of America v. State of Texas* (1981), a school desegregation case that among other things compelled Texas school districts to provide bilingual-bicultural education to limited English proficient students. This law became the basis of a state bilingual law still in existence today.
- *Plyler v. Doe* (1982), a ruling that a Texas law prohibiting state funds for undocumented students violated the equal protection clause of the U.S. Constitution. This ruling was upheld by the U.S. Supreme Court.
- *Keyes v. School District No. 1* (1983), a decision resulting in a Supreme Court ruling that the school district had intentionally segregated Blackde and Latino students, and limited English proficient students suffered significantly due to deficient programming.
- *Comité de Padres de Familia v. Riles* (1979), a California case resulting in a consent decree obligating the state to collect and analyze district data on programs for English learners. The case provided a basis for the state's bilingual education policy for many years.
- *Leticia A. v. Board of Regents* (1985), a California higher education ruling to provide tuition for undocumented students equal to that of resident citizen students.
- *League of United Latin American Citizens (LULAC) et al. v. State Board of Education* (1990), which resulted in a Florida consent decree known as the Multicultural Education, Training and Advocacy (META) Consent Decree (Florida Statute §1003.56), in which every Florida teacher with a limited English proficient student was required to complete 300 hours of in-service training.

And the list goes on for the reader to discover and to marvel at Roos's amazing odyssey. Each story has the feel of a macramé.

One of us (Hakuta) worked with Roos on a small fraction of his portfolio. What he taught then he has shared through this memoir. One important lesson is that legal judgments are part of a larger societal discourse and climate. There is the court of law, the court of public opinion, and the eyes of humanity. The arguments may take a linear form (bilingual education can be effective and should be a remedy for providing meaningful access to English learners), but the context of the societal discourse is distinctively nonlinear and subject to whims—such as a judge deciding to move, a quirky witness, a courageous plaintiff, a sympathetic defendant, an annoying or incompetent opposing counsel. How you win, how you consider the societal climate, and who you identify as fellow travelers in the journey can be just as important as, if not more important than, the judgment itself. Seeming adversaries can turn into important allies.

In this memoir, mostly told in chronological order as Roos emerges from law school in the heady days of the civil rights movement, the story is linear only in the most basic sense of timelines and legal argument. It zips across the multiple advocacy organizations where he worked, criss-crosses geography and levels of government, and paints important lines between the conditions that influence making law, filing lawsuits, and the decision-making through the regulatory process. Most importantly, it is populated by specific people and the culture of specific places.

Throughout the account of the cases, he sprinkles key lessons told frequently in folksy language:

- "While one should search for a perfect solution, you will ruin your chances of obtaining a good solution if you act like a mule" and sometimes it is simply better to "let sleeping dogs lie" if a solution is unrealistic.
- In numerous instances when seeking a remedy, it is valuable to develop it jointly with the local district, as defendants who are "willing to earnestly engage in

developing a remedy ... can provide insights and expertise that outside litigators may lack."

- "The [Supreme] Court's role as the final arbiter of issues with important public policy implications requires the advocate to deeply consider the national, occasionally international, implications of his positions. Pure precedent can never provide all the answers, as is often the case at lower levels."

- Do not overload the meaningfulness of a case as a precedent and choose your priority. In the case of *Plyler v. Doe* (1982), the overriding priority was to secure a meaningful victory for undocumented students. Further consideration of whether education was a "fundamental interest of the state" could overload the case. A strategic choice of considering what kind of win is most desirable could fray the steeliest of nerves, which Roos remedied with long runs and walks in Washington as he prepared for oral argument.

- Do not overreach. "There are times when the wisest course is to let progress proceed organically and not to push for too much too soon."

- "It is important that your case evaluation not be tainted by dislike or dismissal or opposing counsel" lest it interfere with good judgment. And hope that the opposing counsel is competent so that a good argument ensues, thereby solidifying the basis for the victory.

- Be prepared to work with state legislatures and understand the culture, history, and personnel of the system, where you might find unusual allies. And do not hesitate to work within the regulatory and administrative systems where arguments based on theory and research might find a more sympathetic audience.

- Do not oversell a remedy that may be undercut by inadequate implementation. "Mandating native instruction without having teachers capable of delivery is setting yourself up for failure."

- And a salute to the next generation of advocates: "Give youth its due. Oftentimes, it will trump experience."

These and other important lessons are wise counsel for the current law student, educational leader, policy advocate, or scholar as they look at the current state of educational equality.

Indeed, it is easy for a younger generation of advocates to feel deflated about the current state of affairs in America. Today, as back then, the mass media paints a bleak picture of the social and political landscape in the country. However, Roos reminds all of us that that social and political turmoil for minority groups is an ongoing "battle," as he calls it. And, from reading his memoir, we are prompted to think about progress as an upward spiral, constantly circling around similar issues but gradually ascending and building on what has already been established.

Undoubtedly, many of the educational issues Roos and associates tackled over the course of their careers continue to be contested. Debates about affirmative action, voting rights, bilingual education, and school resources are still playing out at the state and federal levels. Nonetheless, progress on these matters is also visible. We have seen how federal legislation has incorporated lessons from a generation of advocates, as detailed in Roos's account. While imperfect, the Every Student Succeeds Act (2015), representing the most recent reauthorization of the Elementary and Secondary Education Act (1965), has once again shed light on English learner students. The creation of new evaluation systems requiring states to judge English learner progress has the potential to hold schools more accountable for this growing student subgroup; an emphasis on parent outreach parallels Roos's takeaways from working together to find solutions; and the provision of grants to encourage more training for teachers who serve English learners echoes the fights in Florida to provide better teacher preparation (*League of United Latin American Citizens (LULAC) et al. v. State Board of Education*, 1990).

As such, Roos's memoir ultimately offers hope and inspiration for advancing educational rights. Through the telling of his career trajectory, we learn just how much has been achieved in the name of racial and linguistic minorities. His story serves as an inspiration for the next generation of idealistic advocates to continue to "think big."

—KENJI HAKUTA
—DIANA MERCADO-GARCIA
Stanford, California

Acknowledgments

The person who provided much of the inspiration for my work, who suffered the most from my long periods away from home and from my occasionally uncharitable behavior, is my wife, Emma Chavez Roos. Thanks for your love and support. Roger Rice could and should write his own version of many of the activities and trends detailed in this memoir. Stefan Rosenzweig, Joe Ortega, Lew Hollman, Irma Herrera, Camilo Pérez, Deborah Escobedo, and many others contributed substantially to the work described here. Kenji Hakuta, Lily Wong-Fillmore, Ricardo Fernandez, and others from the academic world were essential. Finally, Diana Mercado-Garcia provided both intellectual fodder and organizational skill to seeing this book through to fruition. Thanks to all.

Introduction

L ooking for a panacea—that is how it was when I started in 1967. Desegregation and integration were finally coming to America. Earl Warren was chief justice of the United States, and the federally funded Legal Services Corporation, a nonprofit organization established by the U.S. Congress, had a mandate to change the country.

Historical shackles were being broken. Urban riots in Watts, Detroit, and elsewhere were awakening the country to the need for change. Legal tools enacted in 1964 and 1965 provided vehicles for redress,[1] which, when joined with more peaceful avenues of demonstration, seemed destined to change America for the better. In California, the farmworker battles stimulated a broader awareness of discrimination against Chicanos. In Los Angeles, an urban counterpoint in the form of school walkouts awakened a generation.

More generally, university students were on the march—mostly against the Vietnam War, but also against racial injustice. It seemed like the establishment would fall to the historically underserved. The young could be warriors in effecting that fall, especially those who could leverage the legal system. I was privileged to be in that army.

We were incited to think big and to take on issues that could transform. Some went after the welfare system, hoping to change a process that trapped people in poverty and treated people as

---

[1] 42 U.S.C. §2000d prohibited discrimination by any entity receiving federal funds, and 52 U.S.C. §10101 established voting rights.

though they were at fault for their very own poverty. Others took on consumer abuses, which allowed unscrupulous sellers to prey on individuals. Some dealt with housing or voting. To me, a just educational system seemed foundational. One only had to look to the school segregation battles that dominated the press of the day to realize that a just educational system was not what we had.[2] While intentional segregation was an obvious wrong, it was only one of a plethora of discriminatory practices that created an unjust system and assured that children of color would rarely be able to achieve to their capabilities.

While the story told here is in many ways a story of a personal journey, its value is in bearing witness to important historical events. It is a journey that traversed more than 40 years of identifying and battling many of the central barriers that kept Latinos and other children of color from realizing their full potential through the public schools of America. The battles described here were of paramount concern to a community that was emerging from the shadows in the time frame described (1966–2010), and I was privileged to be intimately involved in those battles. It is a history that deserves to be told for whatever lessons can be carried forward.

Carrying forward and updating those lessons will no doubt be a need for a long time to come. We are reminded that Latino and Black segregation is in many ways worse than it was in the 1960s.[3] Whether or not one believes that the cure for segregation should be forced integration, it is hard to deny that today, as in the time of *Brown v. Board of Education of Topeka* (1954), separate is rarely equal for minority students. Now, as then, lower-income Latino and Black students are usually served by less skilled

---

[2] Following *Brown v. Board of Education of Topeka* (1954), which held intentional segregation in schools unconstitutional, lawsuits were filed against virtually every major school district in the country. The pace picked up in the 1960s as it became evident that administrative enforcement was not up to the task of integration.

[3] As of 2013, Black and Latino students were less likely to be in classrooms with White students than in the 1970s and 1980s (Wagner, 2017).

teachers in inferior schools, granted lesser resources, and achieve at much lower levels than their middle-class cohorts. They are expelled at a higher rate, deemed intellectually disabled at a higher rate, and consequently are incarcerated more often—much more often.[4]

The continual need to fight against practices that inevitably flow from segregated schools is apparent to me. Furthermore, hard-won victories invite backlash and efforts to repeal gains made. For example, the battles for linguistically and culturally relevant education for immigrant children need to be fought again, and while it seems legally settled that undocumented students have the right to a core education,[5] vigilantes directly and indirectly thwart that right almost daily somewhere in America. The rights of these students, usually long-term residents of the United States, need be extended so that the youth and indeed all society benefits.

This story is at times chronological, following my personal journey, and at times focuses on substantive areas. At all times it is told from first-hand experiences. While scholars from the solitude of their libraries may drill down deeper and draw highly valuable conclusions from dispassionate observation, this story takes a different track. It attempts to reconstruct battles, and the strategy and context that informed them, from the perspective of someone who was there, who participated in the strategies and who lived the context. Hopefully, this can shed a different light on history as well as provide some insights for those who address educational inequalities in the future.

---

[4] African Americans are incarcerated in state prisons across the country at more than five times the rate for Whites; furthermore, "Latinos are imprisoned at a rate that is 1.4 times the rate of Whites" (Nellis, 2016, p. 3).
[5] This right was established by *Plyler v. Doe* (1982).

1

A Personal Awakening:
The Birth of the California Rural Legal Assistance

I n the spring of 1966, I was a second-year student at the University of California Hastings College of the Law in San Francisco. At the time, an organization known as the Law Students Civil Rights Research Council matched up interested law students with lawyers in the trenches, fighting primarily for racial equality. I applied for a summer position, fully expecting to be in service to those bravely battling discrimination in the Deep South, whose stories were chronicled almost daily in the press.

Instead, a letter arrived from O'Melveny and Myers, a blueblood law firm in Los Angeles, offering me a summer position with an organization that had yet to see the light of day, but which had been awarded a substantial federal grant. Jim Lorenz, a young member of the firm, had parlayed a budding consciousness of farmworker misery to establish a novelty: The California Rural Legal Assistance (CRLA), a statewide law firm that battled rural poverty through the courts. National awareness on this topic had been sparked by *Harvest of Shame* (Friendly, Lowe, & Murrow, 1960), a television documentary presented by broadcast journalist Edward Murrow, and by reports from Delano, California, of a farmworker's strike led by César Chávez, Dolores Huerta, and Larry Itliong. That job offer changed my life as much as CRLA changed the mission of government-funded legal services.

By mid June of 1966, I joined 20 other law students from around the country in a dormitory at the University of Southern

California. We were given several weeks of training in civil rights law, rural poverty, the farmworker movement, and other things long forgotten. The faculty was barely more experienced than the students, with the exception of Gary Bellow, who ran a legal aid clinic at Harvard Law School and was treated as a superstar upon his arrival. In addition to Jim Lorenz, who was energetic and smart but who had no experience delivering legal services to the rural poor, we also had Bob Gnaizda, who would go on to become a disability rights advocate and the founder of Public Advocates, Inc., a public interest nonprofit law firm in San Francisco; Don Kates, who would become better known as a vehement gun rights advocate; Michael "Mickey" Bennett, a CRLA administrator; and Dan Lund, who added a Christian overlay to a Yale legal education.

The University of Southern California presence was all that consisted of CRLA that summer. My job and that of a number of the other students was to go into the field to determine where in California CRLA should place offices. And, relatedly, we were tasked to determine friends, foes, and conditions CRLA might encounter in different locales. It was the most exciting experience of my young life, trying to tie political science and sociological principles to change America through legal advocacy. Whether our youthful research was of any value to the rural poor in general or to CRLA in particular, it nevertheless turned on my light bulb and laid the foundation for a lifetime of law reform work.

CRLA became a beacon of light for legal services around the country. Before CRLA, legal aid organizations helped the poor with divorces, rental disputes, and similar small recurring problems. CRLA, with a nudge from its funders, the directors of the Office of Economic Opportunity, saw its mission as affirmatively challenging underlying conditions that kept the poor and minorities "in their place." Predictably, it angered the political establishment that benefited from the status quo; its fights for survival with Governor Ronald Reagan are well chronicled (Bennett & Reynoso, 1972). CRLA also served as the role model for a number of other Office of Economic Opportunity programs, several of which I had the good fortune of being a part of.

Like most government-funded entities, CRLA and the groups that emulated its aggressiveness were highly dependent on the political winds for maintaining their commitment to change. In 1968, the Nixon administration replaced the Johnson administration. While it was difficult to completely put the law reform genie back in the bottle, government-funded legal programs became increasingly tamer. There was an effort to shield reforms from political shifts by establishing the Legal Services Corporation, which was helpful. But, in general, the most aggressive law reform efforts shifted to privately funded programs in subsequent years, such as the Mexican American Legal Defense Fund, the National Association for the Advancement of Colored People Legal Defense and Education Fund, the American Civil Liberties Union, and other organizations. Multicultural Education, Training and Advocacy, which I was to join in the early 1980s, was one of these, albeit smaller and more specialized than those named above.

2

Los Angeles, 1968–1970

I n December of 1968, word came that I had passed the California bar exam. At the time, I was en route from Miami to New York on a bus after banging around the East Coast following the exam. After Christmas, I headed to Los Angeles to seek my first legal position. Despite family entreaties to look for a good-paying law firm, legal services work of the sort that I had tasted at the California Rural Legal Assistance (CRLA) was what I set my sights on.

It is hard to describe the magnetizing effect of such work without taking into consideration its temporal context. In the several years since my student exposure to CRLA, that organization and other like-minded federally funded legal services programs had found allies in the Washington bureaucracy and in the courts for transformative litigation. Young CRLA lawyers had successfully battled California welfare restrictions that historically would have gone unchallenged (*Morris v. Williams*, 1967). The U.S. Supreme Court had struck down a number of state laws that had been passed to disadvantage consumers (*Sniadach v. Family Finance Corp*, 1969). The fairly dormant commands that no one, including debtors, should be denied due process of the law or equal protection awoke to provide protection for those who lacked political clout. Young, ideologically driven lawyers had led the charge against the sort of overreaching that was commonplace and previously unchallenged. All of this was done with the encouragement of those who oversaw the Legal Services Corporation programs. It was to this environment that many young law school graduates were drawn.

Los Angeles turned out to be a great environment for those wishing to be part of this legal movement. The Watts riots had cast a harsh light on the conditions of African Americans in the city. It came as a surprise to many that a city such as Los Angeles, in which most African Americans lived in single-family houses with grassy front lawns, could contain such a high level of discrimination and misery—a fact that was documented by post-riot studies and exposés.[6]

Similarly, it surprised many who drove through the green farmlands of California that the supposed "paradise" masked the serious misery of those who tended the fields. The conditions exposed by César Chávez and the farmworkers led to an awareness that these ills existed in Los Angeles, the location of the largest concentration of Mexican Americans in the country.

However, the Los Angeles basin was peppered with a number of newly created or energized Legal Services Corporation programs poised to address the ills suffered by African Americans, Latinos, and low-income Whites. Several months after passing the bar exam, I was offered a position as a staff attorney with one of those programs, the Southeast Neighborhood Legal Services (SNLS) program, which had offices in Compton and Norwalk. Compton was adjacent to Watts; the neighborhood was poor and African American, and it was beginning to house an increasing population of Chicanos.

Like many other programs at the time, SNLS was newly minted and predominantly staffed by young, inexperienced White lawyers from some of the better law schools. This was an outgrowth of the fact that minority lawyers were virtually nonexistent at the time, and the salaries would not have attracted minority lawyers who were further along in their careers. Within weeks of my hiring, we would hire Joe Ortega, a slightly older

---

[6] The McCone Commission, appointed by California Governor Pat Brown to identify the causes of the Watts riots, determined that high unemployment, poor schools, and inferior living conditions were the root cause of the riots (California Governor's Commission, 1965).

lawyer with a similar level of legal experience as me, to direct the office in Norwalk.

Although we barely knew how to find the courthouse, the Office of Economic Opportunity pressured SNLS to carry out the law reform mission. With help from the Western Center, which I was to join several years later, Ron Sievers, another young lawyer at SNLS, brought a case which led to a Supreme Court of California ruling that determined prejudgment attachments of property to be unconstitutional.[7]

The School Walkouts

While I tackled a home foreclosure with both litigation and newspaper publicity—thus learning about the value of bringing multiple pressures to bear on a wrongdoer—my most significant initiative requiring legal skills involved schools. It concerned a student strike, which had become a potent tool for educational change in Los Angeles.

It is important to know a little about school finance to understand why student strikes or walkouts became an early strategy to push change. Virtually all school districts in the country receive substantial state funding based upon the number of students they serve. Numbers are computed on a daily head count, typically referred to as average daily attendance. The lower the daily count, the lower the income for school districts. If a district has projected a certain count and opened schools, hired teachers, and otherwise responded to that count, it cannot quickly reduce those costs when the count is suddenly lowered. Thus, a walkout has the potential to get the attention of those who set policy for the schools. It is also good fodder for the press, which similarly can assist with exposing wrongs.

---

[7] Previously, California law had allowed creditors to tie up debtors' possessions and income upon the mere filing of a suit and before its adjudication (*Blair v. Pitchess*, 1971).

Students protest during a walkout at Roosevelt High School, 1968.
From the La Raza Photograph Collection, courtesy of the photographer,
Devra Weber, and the Chicano Studies Research Center.

In the late 1960s, Chicano students from East Los Angeles, supported by sympathetic teachers and community leaders, initiated a number of walkouts. The Compton variation landed at my doorstep, a development I welcomed. The issues in Los Angeles often involved discriminatory educational policies, such as placement of non–English-speaking students into classes for the intellectually disabled. However, the issue in Compton was much more straightforward: students at a predominantly Chicano middle school found themselves as punching bags for high school students who were African American. When some of the high school students got out of school, they would float over to the middle school, which released students a little later in the day. Daily beatings occurred; the middle school students were afraid to attend school and parents responded. With an eye cast toward Los Angeles, Chicano parents decided to withhold their children from school and to demonstrate daily. Compton Unified School District responded by threatening to prosecute parents for interfering with compulsory education laws.

After a weeklong standoff, a school leader invited a group of parents to sit down. Parents felt they needed any legal support I could give, possibly overestimating its value. They insisted that I be part of any negotiations. The school superintendent sought to divide the parents from me by sowing doubt about my commitment. But, the parents did not bite, and negotiations began in earnest. The end product of those negotiations provided lifelong learning: First, while one should search for a perfect solution, you will ruin your chances of obtaining a good solution if you act like a mule. Second, negotiations offer an opportunity for creative thinking; as such, they can be fun. Third, creative thinking ought to involve all of your colleagues. Encouragement should be given to those on the other side of the table to problem-solve. Once drawn in, school administrators can add an invaluable touch. They will know things, hidden to outsiders, that can make the end result more solid.

In the end, the school district agreed to hire and train Chicano staff to monitor the middle school at key hours and to change the release times. This disabled the older students from congregating at the front door of the middle school as it let out. We did not seek suspensions, nor was anyone suspended. The violence died down, kids returned to school, and several individuals who needed employment were put to work. All in all, it was a satisfactory ending. The experience showed me how lawyers can join with parents and activists to address school issues. As a lawyer, I had ways of channeling parent concerns into solutions that might not have otherwise been understandable to school administrators and decision-makers. But, ultimately, it was clear that the political commitment, passion, and experience of the parents and other community activists was foundational.

The Compton walkouts also introduced me to Joaquin Avila, who would go on to be a colleague at the Mexican American Legal Defense Fund (MALDEF), a prominent voting rights attorney, a winner of a MacArthur "Genius Grant" award, and a professor. As it happened, Avila's brother was one of the community activists leading the walkout, and he informed me over beers that he had a brother at Yale University. During a school break, Joaquin and I met. Later, we would touch base at Harvard, where

Joaquin Avila, 1982. Photo courtesy of MALDEF.

he went to law school and where we would work together during the MALDEF years.

MALDEF Comes to California

My second education case was also the first case that MALDEF filed in California. Joe Ortega, my friend and colleague, had left SNLS after being hired to establish a branch office of MALDEF in Los Angeles, for what was then a San Antonio–based civil rights organization. Since Joe gave high priority to eradicating educational discrimination, it was natural to entangle him when a wrong came to my attention.

More than 50 years later, I still remember the names of the two plaintiffs: Johnny Urias, an 18-year-old Chicano, and Robin Wright, his somewhat strapping Anglo classmate. The two were seniors at South Gate High School, which was located in a neighborhood that was changing from working-class White to hard-working, upwardly mobile Chicano. With variations, the scenario we confronted has seemed to play out in virtually all neighborhoods undergoing change.

The two boys, Urias and Wright, had become friends. This seemed to infuriate fellow Anglo students who harassed them until it resulted in a fight, which by today's standards was fairly innocent—no guns, just fists. In hindsight, Los Angeles Unified School District's (LAUSD) response seems to have been predictable. The school district allocated all the blame to Urias and Wright and refused to let the boys attend their graduation ceremony. This was a lesson for me, a middle-class lawyer who had grown up in a family where everyone had gone to college and who would have fled his high school graduation; for students who were the first in their families to graduate from high school, the graduation ceremony was a big deal.

Ortega and I filed to enjoin LAUSD from denying the two boys a place at their graduation ceremony. President and General Counsel of MALDEF Mario Obledo flew out from San Antonio to witness this historic event. As is too often the case, though, we encountered a judge who would not second-guess the schools and who would not attribute racial discrimination without a level of proof virtually impossible to command.

The two boys were not allowed to attend their graduation. Furthermore, something much more ominous occurred. LAUSD sought to punish our clients for bringing the suit by filing criminal charges of battery against the two boys. Feeling responsible for placing the two students in danger of being branded as "criminals," we worked feverishly to have the charges dismissed. We filed a 50-page brief in a criminal court that churned out decisions in factory-like fashion, usually without any paper. The judge, probably motivated more by expedience than by justice, dismissed the charges. We let out a huge sigh of relief. Once again, we learned that when a supposedly liberal institution, such as a school district, has its hegemony challenged, there is a propensity toward ugly retaliation. Teachers, who were our allies in many of our future battles, would consistently encounter this truism.

For those interested in the history of MALDEF, there is a backstory to those early Ortega years. The school walkouts discussed above constituted an important (although not exclusive) theatre of Chicano activism in Los Angeles. Protests—some peaceful, some more edgy—were the order of the day, and criminal charges against activists were frequent. MALDEF, committed primarily to combat the root causes of discrimination, could have devoted all of its scant resources to these minor criminal cases as vocal activists often wished. It took a significant effort by Ortega to fend off these demands, to keep the peace with the activists, and to reserve limited resources for participating in class-type, civil suits, which were more aligned with MALDEF's organizational mission.

One whirlwind that Ortega had to tolerate was an activist lawyer, Oscar Zeta Acosta. Acosta was a brilliant, if eccentric, lawyer at a time when there were only a handful of Chicano attorneys in Los Angeles. He saw his mission as providing unquestioning support to activists, specifically with regard to criminal representation. Although not employed by MALDEF, he muscled his way into the office. Acosta burned white hot, cranking out materials at all times of the day and night. In addition to criminal representation, Acosta found time to challenge the grand jury system in the County of Los Angeles. As part of that lawsuit, he managed to depose a number, if not all, of the Superior Court judges in the county on the grounds that the White, middle-class grand jury was a product of their nominations[8]; this was certainly something that an attorney who thought he would be spending his days in trials before those same judges would have hesitated to undertake. Acosta also ran for district attorney in the county. In the end, Acosta disappeared into Mexico, never to return. In some sense, he was an archetype, albeit extreme, of Chicano lawyers at the time. Maybe you had to be a little crazy to overcome all of the barriers that confronted a Chicano committed to becoming an attorney.[9]

Two and a half years at the SNLS were rewarded with an offer to join the Western Center on Law and Poverty, a regional

---

[8] At the time, the grand jury for the County of Los Angeles was chosen from nominations by California Superior Court judges, virtually all of whom were White.

[9] For more about Acosta, one should read his work, *The Autobiography of a Brown Buffalo* (1972).

legal services center supporting neighborhood-based programs of the Office of Economic Opportunity. Before joining the Western Center, I married Emma Chavez, who had left a teaching career in Mexico to make the big bucks associated with being a Legal Services Corporation receptionist in the Norwalk offices. We married only after surviving a *blitzkrieg* by Ms. Enriquez, my receptionist in Compton. I had earned Ms. Enriquez's bitter hostility by repeatedly admonishing her that her role as a gate-keeper for clients was not to exclude African Americans so that we could see her favored Latino clients.

Our wedding fell on August 29, 1970, the same date of the Chicano Moratorium, one of the largest Chicano demonstrations to occur in Los Angeles during that era. Many of our guests came and went between the reception and the jailhouse. The following day we learned of the death of Ruben Salazar, a famed *Los Angeles Times* columnist, at the hands of the police.[10] Ortega and I had met with Salazar several times, and the loss of the most empathetic *Los Angeles Times* reporter was felt deeply.

With Emma Roos, early 2000.

---

[10] Salazar was killed by a tear gas canister shot by a Los Angeles County sheriff, who allegedly was trying to calm a crowd of protestors. It remains a question whether Salazar was killed accidentally or assassinated.

3

Attacking Multiple Forms of Discrimination:
The Western Center on Law and Poverty Years, 1970–1972

n the 1970s, the Office of Economic Opportunity Legal Services Corporation structure had three levels. There were on-the-ground organizations that mixed service work, such as individual debtor or tenant representation, with some law reform efforts—the Southeast Neighborhood Legal Services (SNLS) fit this mold. At the next level, there were regional centers, which were charged with helping neighborhood programs with technical matters and with law reform initiatives. For example, when Ron Sievers brought a case to us at SNLS (*Blair v. Pitchess*, 1971), he enlisted the Western Center, the regional center for Southern California. The third tier constituted national, subject-based centers. While I have listed the levels as hierarchical, in fact many attorneys preferred the constant contact with real clients, more available via the SNLS programs. Consequently, there was movement among the Legal Services Corporation levels.

When I joined the Western Center, it was heavily populated with individuals who would go on to be professors. These individuals had more of a theoretical bent and were great additions to the array of resources needed to combat institutional wrongs; but, it seemed to me that my experience at the neighborhood level provided invaluable pretraining, which many of them did not have. At the Western Center, I was given a consumer law portfolio, with the promise and freedom to involve myself in education matters. The first major case I landed involved neither, but instead sought to end the disenfranchisement of lawful immigrants. This is a matter that still should be on the agenda of all persons concerned with representative democracy and immigrant rights.

Voting Rights for Noncitizens

In California, and in virtually all U.S. jurisdictions, one must be a citizen to vote. Furthermore, one must meet a certain threshold of English to become a citizen. The effect of these two requirements, especially the first, is to make a mockery of the notion that democracy involves giving the governed power to elect those who do the governing. In the Los Angeles schools, for example, probably more than half of students have parents who are noncitizens and thus cannot vote for the school board that oversees the future of their children.

Two factors convinced us that we might be able to overturn the existing citizenship requirement so as to enable at least permanent residents to vote. First, the U.S. Supreme Court had recently ruled that courts must strictly scrutinize provisions that interfered with the "fundamental right" to vote. Second, research by a very bright, young colleague of mine at the Western Center, Steve Kalish, unearthed evidence that noncitizens had been allowed to vote for most offices in the first century of America's existence. It was only starting in the 1880s, a period of economic downturn and anti-immigrant sentiments, that citizen-only voting provisions became common. Thus, contrary to conventional wisdom, the original understanding did not preclude noncitizen voting.

Kalish and I filed two lawsuits: One challenged the citizenship requirement in state court, and the other challenged the English language provision in federal court. We saw the English requirement as making the transition to citizenship (and political participation) more difficult. We argued, based on California precedent (*Castro v. State of California,* 1970), that English language requirements were based on the false notion that one could not obtain adequate information to participate in the electoral process without speaking English. In California, at least, vibrant newspapers existed in multiple languages.

The state case, even with Kalish's research, was too novel. We took it to a state court of appeal, lost the case, and decided that a California Supreme Court precedent would not help the cause. Better to let sleeping dogs lie, for the present. The federal case took an unusual path: In order to file the lawsuit, it was necessary to have a client who had been denied citizenship because of her language skills.[11] A law clerk at the Western Center had a mother, Mrs. Martínez, who very much wished to be a U.S. citizen and who could meet all of the criteria, except for her English skills. Perfect. Unfortunately, the government learned of our plans before we were able to execute them.

One bright morning, I picked up Mrs. Martínez from her home, and we drove to her appointment at Immigration and Naturalization Services. Surprisingly, when we entered the examination room, we were met by a regional director who was going to administer Mrs. Martínez's oral test personally. It quickly became apparent why Mrs. Martínez had this honor: When asked who George Washington was, a question that would have eluded her in English, she was given prompts that an infant could have picked up. This is how the remainder of the exam went. By the end of the morning, Mrs. Martínez was a citizen, and we had lost a viable client and plaintiff. We probably could have started over, but other matters intervened and this issue faded.

Whether we made the correct decision to abort the state court case could, of course, be questioned. However, it is important that *all* advocates, including attorneys, continually evaluate the consequences of different choices. One should take on an issue only if it is believed victory will be a likely consequence. When

---

[11] Under federal "standing" principles, a plaintiff must receive a benefit from an affirmative ruling by the court.

pushing the envelope, losses are inevitable. But, the consequences of a loss should weigh heavily on all strategic decisions. Losses usually reverberate beyond the immediate situation—and the higher the court, the more serious the effect. A loss from the highest court usually settles a matter for a long time. Furthermore, a loss can embolden hostile forces to enact similar legislation in jurisdictions not bound by the court ruling or to extend the challenged policy beyond the ruling. A loss can also undermine the aura of the attorneys who suffered the loss. With past victories in pocket, government agencies are fairly likely to give deference to winning attorneys and clients, even on other issues. The opposite is true when counsel arrives on a scene with a publicized loss. Yet, even a loss can at times be worth the effort, as the next several cases reflect.

School Conditions

In the early 1970s, as the effort to desegregate schools in Los Angeles began to take root, an awareness developed of the disparities between predominantly Black and Latino schools on the one hand and predominantly White schools on the other. One prominent disparity that surfaced was the differential risk from a possible earthquake.

In the 1930s, an earthquake had rattled the Los Angeles area, causing a school in Long Beach to collapse. Fortunately, the earthquake occurred when classes were not in session. Legislators, realizing that students might not fare as well the next time an earthquake hit, passed a law that set improved building standards for new schools and created a timetable to retrofit the older structures.[12] As is common, more immediate concerns overwhelmed the uncertainty of an earthquake, and the retrofitting requirements were either forgotten or put on a backburner. By the early 1970s, the pre-earthquake schools almost exclusively housed Black and Latino students, as middle-class, White families had

[12] For a current iteration of the Field Act, see California Education Code §17280–17317 and §81130–81147.

migrated out of the city center into suburbs where new earthquake-resistant schools had been built.

However, as a champion of justice, Ortega was there alongside me to correct this wrong. We enlisted the assistance of several luminaries from Caltech's Seismological Laboratory to join us; in fact, my first trip to Las Vegas occurred when I was "forced" to fly there to collect a declaration signature. While we grappled with the courts to find an enforceable remedy, the publicity generated by the lawsuit hastened a commitment by the schools to address the problem. The court ultimately concluded that the matter was not judiciable. At least for a time, the lawsuit provided a jumpstart to renew the retrofitting efforts that had crawled to a halt.

Textbook Adoptions

A second lawsuit involving textbook adoptions in the state was similarly quixotic. California had passed a law that required school textbooks to fairly and nondiscriminatorily represent all racial/ethnic groups.[13] Procedurally, the law required the state to establish expert committees to evaluate how certain groups were treated in textbooks that were being considered for adoption. Subsequently, the committees were to issue analyses that would assist the state in determining which textbook companies should receive contracts.

As we were to discover, textbook adoption in California was not a penny-ante enterprise. A publisher awarded a textbook contract would automatically have orders for hundreds of thousands of books. A decision by a state the size of California could also prompt other states to similarly adopt the textbook. Lastly, if California could assure that a textbook provided fair treatment to all groups, it could help improve representation in textbooks on a national scale.

Perhaps it was inevitable that a panel of people who had spent their professional careers addressing cultural and racial

---

[13] For current law regarding bias in textbook adoptions, see California Education Code §60040 and §60048.

transgressions would in fact identify ample examples in the textbooks they were charged with evaluating. The experts concerned with evaluating the depiction of African Americans found numerous slights, as did the Native American panel, and on through the various committees.

However, the state virtually ignored these findings. Several forces were likely at work. First, awareness of most slights was barely recognizable to an Anglo-centric world in the early 1970s. This was a time when most school districts mistook English language limitations among immigrant children for intellectual disabilities. Second, the pressures by the textbook publishers must have been fierce.

It was into this void that Ortega, from the Mexican American Legal Defense Fund (MALDEF), and I, from the Western Center, stepped into. The work of turning the concerns of the committee members into declarations came to a head shortly before the state was scheduled to sign million-dollar contracts with the textbook publishers. A day of flying around the state getting signatures on declarations ended in a Sacramento courthouse on a Friday afternoon. Our declarations and papers overmatched the attorney general. By the end of the day, we had, albeit temporarily, received a court order barring the signing of the contracts.

The injunction sent tremors throughout the textbook industry. Thirty days later, when the matter returned to court, we confronted not only the attorney general's staff but a slew of lawyers from prestigious East Coast law firms. In retrospect, the opposing counsel's argument was predictable, but it was unanticipated by us as young lawyers. They argued forcefully that the First Amendment provision with regard to the freedom of speech would be violated if the injunction was extended, and the judge agreed.

There is no doubt in my mind that the legislation, supported by our litigation, was worth the effort. The stereotypes found in school textbooks, which were given the official stamp of approval by the state, had to be addressed. However, this is not to say that courts should not be cautious. We have seen special interest groups on the right promoting their views on abortion, global warming, and other matters into textbooks.[14] The left is no less likely to attempt this type of influence in textbooks, given a heartfelt (or ideological) desire to provide the "right" education to children. Textbooks should not shy away from controversial subjects, but oversight of racial/ethnic and gender slights ought to be ongoing.

Desegregation in California

The biggest case I handled during this period involved Oxnard School District in California in *Soria v. Oxnard School District Board of Trustees* (1971). At the time, Oxnard was a farming community that was deeply divided by race. Most Mexican farmworkers and their families lived on one side of Oxnard Boulevard, while growers and Anglos lived on the other. Our analysis showed a pattern in Oxnard that mirrored patterns in other communities that had been the subject of desegregation complaints.[15] Superficially, the schools were segregated because housing was segregated, but closer examination showed that the school district did all it could to maintain such a pattern.

Rather than building schools near the racial dividing line to enhance integration, the district built schools in the far reaches of each community. Whenever logic suggested that an existing school should be integrated, boundaries were altered to avoid that outcome. When a White child was "trapped" in a school serving Mexican students, "opportunity transfers" allowed them to exit.

In filing this case, we had the good fortune of drawing a sympathetic arbiter, federal Judge Harry Pregerson. Using facts and the law, we were able to proceed summarily without a full trial. The judge agreed with our argument and, after considering detailed written evidence, ordered Oxnard to desegregate its

---

[14] In particular, Texas has been on the cutting edge of textbook battles (Perera, 2014).
[15] For example, see *Keyes v. School District No. 1* (1969) and *Davis v. School District of City of Pontiac, Inc.* (1970).

schools (*Soria v. Oxnard School District Board of Trustees,* 1971). It was one of the first Chicano desegregation rulings in California since the 1940s.[16]

The Oxnard decision was followed by an all-out barrage to stay its implementation pending appeal. After several rejected requests to justices of the U.S. Supreme Court, the U.S. Congress passed the Bloomfield Amendment (1972), one of the early anti-desegregation laws. The amendment specifically stayed cases on appeal. The Nixon Justice Department joined Oxnard School District in seeking a stay from the Ninth Circuit based upon the amendment's provisions. National attention turned to Oxnard, triggering the appearance of segregationist Florida Governor Claude Kirk. Arguing to a packed Ninth Circuit courtroom, we prevailed on the theory that our ruling preceded passage of the amendment.[17] In making this argument, we were able to tap into national resources such as the National Association for the Advancement of Colored People Legal Defense and Education Fund (NAACP LDF) for support.

Despite everything, desegregation occurred without major incident. The most telling recollections I have from those days were calls from members of the Mexican community in awe at the newfound cleanliness and sparkling equipment at the formerly White schools that were now compelled to accept Mexican children. For me, it reaffirmed the belief that desegregation was much more than a theoretical righting of wrongs.

It is worth noting that, the following year, U.S. Supreme Court decisions cast doubt on the use of summary procedures in desegregation cases. The case was retried. In the retrial, evidence from school board minutes was introduced dispelling any notion that the segregation of the Oxnard schools was innocent.

A final education case I tried with Ortega involved busing, a variation on the desegregation battles. The late 1960s and early

---

[16] Earlier cases included "The Lemon Grove Incident" (1931), *Mendez v. Westminister School District* (1946), and *Romero v. Weakley* (1955).

[17] This is in reference to *Soria v. Oxnard School District Board of Trustees* (1972).

1970s were the heyday of school desegregation, and these busing cases were being fought all over the country. A number of school districts, sometimes in recognition of their vulnerability and sometimes in good faith, decided to get a jump on the courts. Unfortunately, racial bias often infected the process—thus giving rise to cases challenging one-way busing.

These busing cases were very difficult to win. My first case involving these matters also happened to be my last case at the Western Center, and it involved the Fullerton schools. Following a traditional pattern, the Fullerton School District in Orange County chose to integrate by closing an older, poorly maintained school that primarily served Chicano students. It then proposed busing Mexican children to the underutilized, newer, and spiffier schools serving White students. While Chicano parents were not hostile to desegregation, the notion that they had to give up their neighborhood school and go across town seemed unfair. Indeed, it was not only unfair in terms of commuting time; there was evidence that the bused kids were treated as unwanted strangers.

School districts had a number of built-in defenses to which White judges were usually receptive. First, the school district would wrap itself in a cloak of integration: Why should we be punished for doing right? This was their lament. Further, they could argue that the minority children were escaping an inferior facility—failing to note, of course, that they were responsible for such a disparity. Finally, by closing an inferior, overcrowded school and filling an underused facility, the school district saved resources. Who does not value frugality?

In any event, we challenged Fullerton's one-way busing plan. After we lost the case, I remember our opposing counsel conceding that she might have ruled differently than the judge. Be that as it may, the decision was mainstream—although the same antic following a finding of *de jure* segregation was occasionally struck down.

Although the Nixon ascension to the presidency in 1968 was a strike against racial integration, the courts really did not put on the brakes until a U.S. Supreme Court ruling in 1974, *Milliken v.*

Bradley. National battles were mirrored in California with certain twists. In the late 1960s, a state court ruled that *de facto* segregation was actionable in California. This ruling, which would have led to the desegregation of Los Angeles, was promptly met by the electoral defeat of the judge who made the ruling and by the passage of a constitutional amendment in 1972 requiring a finding of intentional or *de jure* segregation before desegregation could be forced by the courts (*Crawford v. Los Angeles Board of Education,* 1982). Thus, following these occurrences, only Oxnard and a few other jurisdictions were subject to court orders.

This is not to say that much of the segregation we see today is innocent, only that the burden of proving intent became too high. Further, as in other areas of the country, divisions popped up among Black and Chicano populations with regard to the desirability of desegregation. As I describe later, the Chicano community was especially ambivalent. By the mid 1970s, concerns about Black pride in the African American community and about preservation of nascent bilingual programs in the Chicano community tended to put a lid on efforts that the courts had already begun to erode.

4

Moving On:
Center for Law and Education
at Harvard

My experience at the Western Center increased my appetite for a venue where I could expand my educational involvement. Fortunately, the scaffolding created by programs of the Office of Economic Opportunity's Legal Services Corporation included a number of specialized centers affiliated with prominent universities. These centers were designed to blend academic research with civil rights advocates with the goal of improving conditions for the disadvantaged. Most of the programs engaged in litigation, usually in partnership with a local neighborhood program. For example, there was a center specializing in welfare law at Columbia University, a center specializing in housing at the University of California, Berkeley, and a consumer law project at Boston College.

In the fall of 1972, I was offered a position at the Center for Law and Education (CLE) at Harvard by the director, Marian Wright Edelman, who would move on to found the Children's Defense Fund. The CLE was funded by the federal government, but it was sponsored by Harvard Law School and the Harvard Graduate School of Education. Nick Flannery, a former senior attorney for the Civil Rights Division of the Department of Justice, was the director of litigation. In addition, CLE hired a handful of attorneys, including Roger Rice, with whom I would later found Multicultural Education, Training and Advocacy (META).

My wife, Emma, and I drove across the country in our Volkswagen camper with our cat Pimiento. In mid November of 1972, the first snow of the season fell just as we crossed into Massachusetts. We were grounded in the Berkshires; it was magical, though we would soon learn that fresh snow turns to grime fairly quickly in the city.

Our first weekend in Cambridge, I coaxed Emma into attending the annual Harvard–Yale football game. Sitting in the Yale rooting section of the stadium, surrounded by captains of industry chanting "Bulldog! Bulldog! Bow, wow, wow!" helped break the awe associated with being in the bowels of the Ivy League. Staying with acquaintances in Plymouth for Thanksgiving also provided us with a sense of continuity, as local Native Americans demonstrated against the devil colonists. It felt like California.

During my tenure, the CLE handled a number of nationally prominent cases. Indeed, the Boston desegregation case, *Morgan v. Hennigan* (1974), began soon after I arrived. It gobbled up Flannery and several other attorneys for most of my time at the center. The Molly Hootch case (*Hootch v. Alaska State-Operated School System*, 1975) broke the practice of forcing young Native Americans to attend debilitating boarding schools.[18] With the litigation coming fortuitously at the time oil was discovered, hundreds of schools were built in the Alaskan hinterlands. Roger Rice (more on him later) laid the groundwork for turning *U.S. v. Texas* (1981) into a statewide bilingual case, which I would later co-lead with him. Flannery also unsuccessfully argued in the U.S. Supreme Court that Detroit desegregation should include the White suburbs (*Milliken v. Bradley*, 1974). This loss, a reflection of the turning tide in courts, marked the beginning of the end of the desegregation movement.

I found myself as the lead attorney in two cases—one that would result in a U.S. Supreme Court victory, and the other that would alter services for disabled students in Rhode Island. I also

---

[18] For more information about this case, see review by Cotton (1984).

co-counseled another one-way busing loss in Stamford, Connecticut, and I began my collaboration with Rice in Texas.

Boston in the 1970s was a place with a schizophrenic personality when it came to race. Emma and I arrived in Massachusetts at a time when it had the unique distinction of being the only state in the country to vote for the Democratic presidential candidate, Senator George McGovern. Furthermore, seated right in front of our apartment was a statue of William Lloyd Garrison, a prominent abolitionist and leader in the movement to free slaves via the underground railroad. These and other things would suggest, if not a utopia, a place of racial tolerance. At the CLE, though, I had a front row seat to another version of Boston. The CLE was counsel for African American plaintiffs in the Boston desegregation case (*Morgan v. Hennigan,* 1974), which exposed some of the ugliest racial backlash encountered by those seeking school integration (not excluding Alabama and Mississippi).

The First Bilingual Law and Its Questionable Implementation

This schizophrenia became further evident to me as a result of pillow talk with my wife. Emma had secured a teaching job in Cambridge during the first year of a mandated bilingual program. The program was the first of its kind in the country, and it was the product of legislation drafted by attorneys at the CLE. The legislation envisioned expanded access to school offerings in Massachusetts. However, what Emma revealed to me was diametrically the opposite of this.

In her school, Kennedy-Longfellow, as in other Cambridge schools, if you graduated from the eighth grade, you had a choice of attending an academic high school or a trade school. If you did not receive a diploma, there was no choice: you went to the trade school, which pretty much precluded a college education. Emma indicated that the students who had participated in the bilingual program at Longfellow were not deemed to have exhibited the skills needed to graduate. Thus, they received a certificate of completion and a one-way pass to the trade school.

Long story short, we threatened to sue. After some pushback and negotiations, Cambridge Public Schools agreed to hold a special graduation for the predominantly Latino children who had been denied participation in the regular graduation. Since Latinos constituted an emerging political block, every politician with ambitions spoke at this graduation, praising the children for being pioneers. But, there was no mention of why the graduation ceremony was taking place in July. This event reminded me that the wisdom in some of the most prestigious universities on the planet did not necessarily spill over into the communities in which they were housed.

Our collaboration on this issue also shed a light on a heretofore unknown side of my wife. During the time she was in Cambridge, Emma became a leader of the Hispanic community. She carried this passion of justice for Latino youth to Oakland, where we moved after Boston and where we have spent much of our lives.

Having come off a nationally significant desegregation victory in Oxnard, it was natural that Edelman, director of the CLE at Harvard, envisioned that I would participate in several desegregation cases in which the center was involved. Two desegregation cases, one in Dayton (*Dayton Board of Education v. Brinkman*, 1979) and another in Columbus (*Columbus Board of Education v. Penick*, 1979), were on the eve of trial, while a third case was still in a preliminary stage (*Alvarado v. El Paso ISD*, 1979).

I was unable to join Harvard's CLE in time to work on the Dayton desegregation case, but I was able to reestablish a linkage with the Mexican American Legal Defense Fund (MALDEF), which had taken on *Alvarado v. El Paso ISD* (1979). My work on this case involved helping build the record and serving as a punching bag for a federal judge who was a longstanding citizen of El Paso. Each court appearance I made left me feeling like I was a participant in a play that had been already written. When faced with a judge who was part of the establishment in that isolated

Texas town, an outsider had little chance of success. Apart from building the case, I was able to visit El Paso and Juarez where Emma had family. We regularly replenished our larder and brought back tortillas, chilies, and other fixings for Mexican dishes for our Chicano friends and students at Harvard. In 1974, the only tortillas available in Boston came in cans from, of all places, "Old El Paso." Laying the foundation for the trial in El Paso, which Avila (now a Harvard graduate) passed to me after I joined MALDEF, was only a modest part of my docket at Harvard's CLE. Several other cases deserve discussion.

Discipline and Due Process: *Goss v. López*

It turned out that more was happening in Ohio than desegregation. Soon after I arrived at Harvard's CLE, a situation involving mass school suspensions of Black students in Columbus found its way to my desk. As was not uncommon in the early 1970s—and mirroring what I had seen in Los Angeles—Black students at one of the secondary schools had invited a Black activist from Ohio State University to speak at a school event. Predictably, the administration stepped in and prohibited the event, leading to a peaceful demonstration that spread to a number of other schools in the district. Using state law, the administration then suspended every student it suspected of participating without hearings. As it turned out, being Black resulted in suspension. Thus, for example, one girl who was on her way home after school had been closed was given a 10-day suspension for "walking out."

Dennis Murphy, a Columbus attorney in private practice who was consulting with the local branch of the American Civil Liberties Union, contacted us at Harvard's CLE. A lawsuit was filed challenging the suspensions on the grounds of due process, and I was asked to try the case.

At the time, there were no U.S. Supreme Court rulings on the subject of school expulsions or suspensions. Furthermore, there were few laws discussing the need for a hearing preceding a suspension. In my arguments at the trial level and then before the

U.S. Supreme Court, I concluded that it was necessary to show that seemingly well-meaning school officials could be wrong and biased, and, secondly, that even a short-term suspension could have life-altering effects.

At the trial, it was clear that young Black students were singled out for being Black. Testimony showing the mindlessness of many of the suspensions met my first condition. With respect to harm, we enlisted Herbert Rie, a psychologist affiliated with Ohio State University, to testify. He concluded that the imposition of an undeserved penalty on a young person had the potential to create feelings of powerlessness, which could have lasting effects. Further, when apparent racial discrimination was involved, feelings of racial inferiority or hostility to a White-controlled system could be expected consequences. The students themselves reinforced these conclusions while establishing their innocence of any wrongdoing.

A three-judge federal court struck down the Ohio statute that allowed these arbitrary suspensions in *López v. Williams* (1974). But the U.S. Supreme Court accepted the appeal of Ohio, so we were off to the races. The first question that popped into our minds was: Who should handle the U.S. Supreme Court work? We were now at a stage that could affect national policy.

Sometimes, there are battles between co-counsel, either seeking glory or having an enhanced value of their worth. That was not the case here. Rather, as the lead counsel at the trial level, I had 6 or 7 years of experience under my belt, but limited appellate experience. Flannery, the director of litigation at the CLE, was seasoned. He had just argued *Milliken v. Bradley* (1974), the Detroit desegregation case, before the U.S. Supreme Court. Using objective measures, Flannery was the logical choice to argue the case.

When presented with the choice, though, Flannery insisted that I take the case to fruition. His argument: You are committed to the case. You built it up. You are capable. Taken together, these outweigh experience. Using this analysis as a springboard, I worked my tail off in a way that a more experienced advocate

The Supreme Court in 1975, at the time of *Goss v López*. Left to right in the front row is Justice Potter Stewart, Justice William O. Douglas, Chief Justice Warren E. Burger, Justice William J. Brennan Jr., and Justice Byron R. White. In the back row is Justice Lewis Powell Jr., Justice Thurgood Marshall, Justice Harry A. Blackmun, and Justice William H. Rehnquist. Photo: Getty Images/Bettmann.

would likely have foregone. Indeed, on the day of the argument, the most experienced U.S. Supreme Court civil rights attorney of the day had another case on the docket. Several knowledgeable observers commented on the disparate preparation that seemed to have gone into our arguments. The lesson: Give youth its due. Oftentimes, it will trump experience.

However, a dilemma arose as I put the case together for the U.S. Supreme Court, one that confronts most litigators at that level. There is substantial pressure from advocates to ask for more than is likely to make sense to the Court. But, if one argues that the ideal is all that can satisfy the legal standard, the Court may reject a lesser alternative that is far superior to a loss. The dilemma manifested itself in *Goss v. López* (1975) with the urging by some to argue for a full-blown hearing—even though we were dealing with short-term suspensions. Some claimed that a hearing that did not include the full panoply of due process (e.g., a neutral judge, right to counsel, evidentiary rules, right to appeal) would continue the arbitrariness. While sharing these concerns, it seemed to me that some due process was a step forward in these situations, that a loss was virtually certain if the Court felt it had an all-or-nothing situation, and that a loss could lessen the effort to bring many of these same protections to more serious penalties. Conversely, a victory would strengthen the hand of advocates.

I believe the reality has been much as I predicted. Students facing short-term suspensions have improved but imperfect protections against error and arbitrariness. Fuller protections have evolved when there are sterner penalties. In any event, our victory in *Goss v. López* (1975) was by a 5-4 margin (showing how close we were to a loss).

Education for the Disabled

Following a short respite, I returned to what was one of my more difficult cases—although it was also one filled with many learning opportunities. In the early 1970s, there were virtually no legislative protections for the disabled. However, there was a burgeoning legal effort, often spearheaded by attorneys who had disabled family members, to bring some justice to this population.

Our entrance into an oversized fight in Rhode Island occurred in an unusual fashion. A Rhode Island attorney with an autistic child, at wits end, filed a lawsuit against the state to have it pick up the bill for educating and responding to his child's condition. The federal judge to whom the case was assigned, Raymond Pettine, had unusual sensors for a significant case. Feeling that the counsel representing the child could use some help, Pettine referred them to Rhode Island Legal Services, an Office of Economic Opportunity–funded organization in the mold of CRLA. As they had little expertise in education litigation, Rhode Island Legal Services picked up the phone and called Harvard's CLE. Being new to the CLE and thus without a full docket, I was assigned to the case.

The Rhode Island case, to be known as *Rhode Island Society for Autistic Children (RISAC) v. Board of Regents* (1975), led to a firestorm of lobbying by advocates for varied disabled groups in the state. Each group argued that their efforts would continue to be ignored unless we took up their cause. Since I was young, dumb, and a bleeding heart to boot, the case came to encompass issues that went well beyond the education of autistic children. Before we were finished, our class included every disabled child in Rhode Island, including those in juvenile facilities and hospitals. It encompassed education and training for children with physical, mental, or psychological disabilities. It also came to include those who had been classified as disabled through imperfect screening systems, who should not have been in disabled programs. At the time, many children who were seen as different were labeled "educable mentally retarded" and delivered an abbreviated educational program.

Almost unwittingly, I was able to enlist virtually every respected academic in the state to support the lawsuit. These commitments were often made before the state gained traction, thus making it more difficult for the state to put pressure on these key people to support *their* case. Their support was of immeasurable help when the case ultimately went to trial. Nevertheless, the trial proved difficult, even with a sensitive judge. Our preliminary discovery filled an entire room in the federal courthouse. It was difficult to keep issues, evidence, and remedies clear. Some of these problems would have become lessened with modern technology—or in the hands of an attorney who was a more natural trial lawyer.

Nevertheless, the Rhode Island case taught me that there is value in minimizing, as much as possible, the complexity of litigation. Most significant civil rights cases are concerned with institutional change, which, by definition, encompasses complex liability and remedial issues. The attorney who lives with a case for several years may think he grasps each of its strands, but he must continually give himself a reality check. Immersion can do funny things to one's mind, including the delusion that a questionable point is both certain and winnable. Of even greater danger, it is not fair nor reasonable to expect that a judge hearing the evidence for the first time will understand the nuances that you have come to appreciate over the years. Yes, sometimes it will be necessary to fight a single fight with multiple strands and complexities. Yet it is almost always worth the effort to streamline your case; victory and actual implementation are more certain when you do.

After approximately 6 weeks of trial, we adjourned to the Rhode Island State House, where the governor's office and other state officials were drawn into a complex negotiation to resolve the case. A consent decree ensued, which rearranged hunks of Rhode Island's delivery system for disabled children.

Beginnings of Rice and Roos

I first met Roger Rice when interviewing for a position at the CLE. He had just returned from a fact-finding trip in California, and he impressed me with his knowledge of cases and movements in my own backyard. At the time, Rice spoke in glowing terms of meeting José Cárdenas, a Texas educator, and he additionally spoke of the potential of using a statewide desegregation case, *U.S. v. Texas* (1971), to advance bilingual education, which was still only an idea floating in the heavens. It is also worth noting that even though we were at the CLE during the same time, our paths rarely crossed.

For most of my time at Harvard's CLE, I again had few dealings with Rice. He was immersed in a case, *Black Voters v. McDonough* (1976), which sought to alter the composition of the Boston school board. Ironically, when he finally got to trial, Rice was aided by a recent recruit, Stefan Rosenzweig, whom I had met in California and had just recommended for a position. When Rosenzweig arrived, I was working on the cases described above so we did not cross paths. As with Rice, though, Rosenzweig and I would share a number of initiatives in the ensuing years.

With the closure of *RISAC v. Board of Regents* (1975), I accepted leadership of the educational advocacy program at MALDEF in San Francisco. While at MALDEF, and subsequently at META, Rice and I became a team known as "Rice and Roos" or "Roos and Rice."

5

MALDEF, 1976–1982

After I left California in the fall of 1972, much had occurred at the Mexican American Legal Defense Fund (MALDEF). It had moved its national office from San Antonio to San Francisco, fleeing a city that had a substantial Chicano population and which also housed Henry B. González, the most prominent Chicano legislator of his time who was often angered by MALDEF activism. San Francisco, with a much smaller Chicano population, seemed a likely refuge from the divisive internecine wars that were occurring in San Antonio. Los Angeles, a city in which MALDEF had already established a beachhead, had been rejected because it had much of the volatility of San Antonio.

In the interim, Vilma Martínez had replaced Mario Obledo as president of the organization. While both Martínez and Obledo were Texans, Martínez had an Ivy League education and New York experience, which she was putting to use to further professionalize MALDEF.

To my sadness, on the eve of my return to California, I received a call from Deputy Mayor of Los Angeles Grace Davis urging me to counsel my old sidekick, Joe Ortega, back from despair. Ortega stood accused of soliciting a minor; he had gone on from MALDEF to become the first Chicano on California's Agricultural Labor Relations Board, which was charged with refereeing the battles between César Chávez's United Farm Workers and California farm growers. Given the hostility of the growers to the board and the perceived bias of Ortega toward the union, it is not far-fetched to believe that he might have been set up. In any event, he pleaded no contest, accepted a short stay in a

In San Francisco in the 1990s.

psychiatric prison facility, and was suspended from practicing law for several years. Years later, he would join me as co-counsel on *Rodríguez v. Los Angeles Unified School District (LAUSD)* (1992).

Affirmative Action Admissions: *Regents of the University of California v. Bakke*

Almost before I had found my office at MALDEF, the first major challenge to affirmative action landed on my desk. Allan Bakke had repeatedly and unsuccessfully sought admission at the University of California, Davis School of Medicine. Bakke suspected that a system that set aside specific slots for Blacks and Chicanos was blocking his entrance, and he was right. During pre-trial discovery, his legal team uncovered evidence that he would have been admitted had it not been for a strict affirmative action quota.

Since I had spent 9 years of my professional life focused on issues closer to the education of low-income and disadvantaged students, I was forced to educate myself about affirmative action. I was surprised that I felt some unease about affirmative action, which somehow felt different than the battles directly confronting discrimination. However, study convinced me that MALDEF's position, which stated that affirmative action was a necessary tool to help discriminated groups overcome decades of discrimination, was correct. As President Lyndon B. Johnson (1965) said in a speech delivered at Howard University:

> You do not take a person who, for years, has been hobbled by chains and liberate him, bring him up to the starting line of a race and then say, "You are free to compete with all the others," and still justly believe that you have been completely fair.

I came to the *Bakke v. Regents of the University of California* (1976) case just after the Supreme Court of California had struck down the University of California, Davis plan. The ruling had been narrow and, of course, was limited to California, at least in theory. This led to a conundrum: Should we urge the defendant in the case, which was the University of California, to appeal to the U.S. Supreme Court? Or, should we work with the ruling of the California courts?

After intense discussions with state and national advocacy organizations for disadvantaged groups as well as with student and faculty groups in California, a decision was made to urge the University of California to accept defeat and remake its affirmative action effort along lines allowed by the Supreme Court of California. Contributing to this view was skepticism that the University of California, which would be the primary defender of the policy, would in fact be a forceful advocate for affirmative action. This was fed by a feeling that the University of California had not done its best in the California courts.

The regents' decision to appeal was made in the glare of intense national publicity, primarily because MALDEF, the National Association for the Advancement of Colored People Legal Defense and Education Fund (NAACP LDF), and other groups were urging the university not to appeal. Notwithstanding our unified demand, the regents voted to seek review. I participated in one brief urging the U.S. Supreme Court not to take the case. This surprising turn of events may have contributed to the Court's decision to grant review, despite the fact that it was increasingly conservative.

Our efforts at this point turned on pressuring the University of California to present the best case possible. Given the national stature of MALDEF and the other affected organizations, the University of California gave us unusual access as they proceeded. Partially to assuage our concerns that the university's legal staff had not shown it was up to the task of arguing this momentous case, the regents agreed to hand the argument over to Harvard Professor Archibald Cox, the former U.S. solicitor general who had earned universal acclaim for standing up to President Richard Nixon during the Watergate scandal several years before.

Boxcars of amicus briefs in support of the university were generated, and I participated in several. In the end, the U.S. Supreme Court issued a ruling in *Regents of the University of California v. Bakke* (1978), which was about the best that we could have hoped for. While ruling that strict affirmative action quotas were unconstitutional, the Court gave its blessing to Harvard University's approach, which considered race along with other factors in shaping its admissions policy. The U.S. Supreme Court was unwilling to second-guess the most prestigious universities in the land, which had long held that diversity was a high value in shaping admissions. This decision led to a collective sigh of relief and renewed efforts to amend policies to meet the Court's objections, as well as decades of further efforts to pare back the ruling in *Regents of the University of California v. Bakke* (1978)—efforts that are still ongoing.[19]

One of the major arguments we advanced in our brief was that Chicano and Black graduates were more likely to return to their respective communities to provide medical services to

---

[19] For more about ongoing efforts, see *Grutter v. Bollinger* (2003) and *Fisher v. University of Texas* (2013).

groups that were vastly underserved. In addition, compelling evidence was presented that cultural and linguistic attributes came into play when addressing medical needs. It was argued that doctors who were products of disadvantaged communities were more likely to address these unique needs. Having lived much of my life working and socializing with communities of color, my experience reinforces what we argued in *Bakke v. Regents of the University of California* (1976). Minority graduates are often drawn by the promise to assist their community, which is generally underserved by professionals. This is true whether we are speaking of medicine, law, or other professions.

My early days at MALDEF were also notable for the relationship I developed with José Cárdenas and his staff at the Intercultural Development Research Association in San Antonio. It turned out that Rice had been correct in singling out Dr. Cárdenas, also known as "The Doc," as a crucial player in the fight for educational equity in Texas and across the nation. Cárdenas had fallen tantalizingly short in putting together an effort to reform educational financing in Texas. He had thrown his intellectual weight and research abilities behind *San Antonio Independent School District v. Rodríguez* (1973), in which the U.S. Supreme Court in a 5-4 ruling refused to strike down a school finance scheme that allowed rich local school districts to generate much higher financial support for students residing therein. "The Doc's" persistence on this subject was to ultimately pay off in a case to be discussed later.

Cárdenas was not a one-issue advocate, however. He had assisted Department of Justice attorneys in convincing Judge William Justice, a sympathetic federal U.S. District Court jurist in East Texas, to include a language remedy as part of a desegregation plan involving two South Texas school districts (*U.S. v. Texas*, 1971). Believing that linguistic and cultural barriers were major causes of school failure among Mexican Americans, Cárdenas sought to find a way to use Judge Justice's ruling to address those issues more broadly. With Cárdenas' urging, Rice and MALDEF had identified the statewide desegregation case, *U.S. v. Texas* (1971), as a vehicle to do this.

The Bilingual Education Movement: *U.S. v. Texas*

The *U.S. v. Texas* (1981) case was to occupy me, as well as Rice, Cárdenas, and the Intercultural Development Research Association team, from my opening days at MALDEF to well after I left the organization in 1982. Our goal was to secure a statewide order compelling Texas school districts to provide bilingual-bicultural education to all limited English-speaking Chicanos in the state. But, first, a brief overview of the bilingual education movement, which was the primary Chicano civil rights issue in education for almost two decades.

Looking back, both the legal and the educational roots of the bilingual education movement were somewhat muddied. The earliest legal expression occurred in the 1968 rewrite of the Elementary and Secondary Education Act,[20] which merely enabled school districts to apply for federal funds to respond to the needs of limited English proficient (LEP) students[21]; no particular strategy was compelled. Then, in 1972, the Office for Civil Rights (OCR) of what was then the U.S. Department of Health, Education, and Welfare—later, the U.S. Department of Education—issued the "May 25 Memorandum," requiring school districts with a nucleus of English learner students to respond to their needs. Again, this was done without specifying what satisfied the law (35 Fed. Reg. §11595, 1970). This announcement followed on the heels of a study of Mexican American school failure by the U.S. Commission on Civil Rights (1971). In 1974, the May 25 Memorandum was declared law by a unanimous U.S. Supreme Court decision in *Lau v. Nichols* (1974). The Court itself noted that the memorandum did not take pedagogical sides on what was legally mandated; affirmative steps were required.

---

[20] See 20 U.S. Code §6301, specifically Title III.
[21] LEP students are now commonly referred to as English language learners (ELL) or English learners (EL).

Following *Lau v. Nichols* (1974), the OCR convened a panel of experts whose *de facto* leader was Dr. Cárdenas. In 1975, it injected for the first time a circuitous mandate for a particular approach, transitional bilingual education (TBE). The mandate is described as circuitous, because the document that emerged from the panel, the Lau Remedies, was issued with the understanding that it only become a mandate if the affirmative steps required were first found to have been violated, which constituted a violation of Title VI of the 1964 Civil Rights Act by way of *Lau v. Nichols* (1974). As described later, I was at the center of an ill-fated effort to have a variation of the Lau Remedies become a direct federal mandate rather than merely a remedy for a violation of the May 25 Memorandum. While all of this federal law was developing, states were already weighing in. In 1972, Massachusetts passed the Transitional Bilingual Education Law, the first transitional bilingual mandate; California followed suit with the Chacón-Moscone Bilingual-Bicultural Education Act of 1976, and several other states enacted similar variations.[22]

I will describe the role I played on the legal roller-coaster that culminated with several state propositions, supported by Ron Unz in the 1990s, that more or less put a lid on bilingual or native language instruction, while leaving untouched the affirmative steps mandate of *Lau v. Nichols* (1974). This legal roller-coaster must be understood against a backdrop of the different affirmative steps that various Latino (and, in some instances, Asian) educational advocates favored.

The most straightforward and modest effort was a program that essentially focused all attention on teaching English. An English as a second language (ESL) program might offer a bit of supplemental help to a child in her native language, but that was all. ESL was, and is, considered a bedrock obligation under federal law—a step up from this was TBE. Pedagogically, TBE offers a full program in the child's native language coupled with a vigorous

---

[22] For more information, see examples in Illinois (105 ILCS 5/14 C-3) and New Jersey (NJSA 18a: 35-16).

ESL program. Entitlement to participate in such a program is based on the inability to make progress in an English-only program, but this entitlement disappears when the student acquires sufficient English to compete with his native English-speaking peers. The Lau Remedies, various state laws, and several court orders we secured were based on TBE. During the heyday of the movement, there were also advocates for maintenance programs. The philosophical basis of maintenance was the belief that language choice in schools should be a parental right, and if parents wanted their child educated in the home language—irrespective of the child's skill—they should have that right. To my knowledge, this was never embodied in a law, yet many advocates viewed anything less as cultural imperialism. In recent years, dual language programs have become popular. These programs purport to teach English language learner students English while teaching native English speakers a second language. They are adopted with incentives, but they are not mandated by schools.

The litigation that preoccupied much of my time sought TBE. Our theory, stated in different ways depending on the legal authority, was that equal or meaningful access to academic content could not be secured if you were teaching children in a language they could not understand. All TBE advocates, whether in court or elsewhere, coupled this argument with a claim for an effective ESL program alongside TBE. At times, we got both. At other times, due to the ambivalence of the federal law, we only got the latter—or, we lost cases, because ESL but not TBE was already in place.

While there have been several legal efforts to secure bilingual education in courts, the most ambitious was our joust with Texas. We were prompted by Judge Justice's ruling in a statewide desegregation case (*U.S. v. Texas*, 1971); the desegregation remedy stated that two border school districts should also include a language component. Rice had devised a strategy to convert this desegregation case into a bilingual case, and that effort was awaiting development as I joined MALDEF.

There was somewhat of a built-in tension between civil rights advocates for bilingual education and those who sought to maintain their language as a state-supported right. From a civil rights viewpoint, monolingual education denied equal access to schooling to those who did not speak the language of instruction. Thus, bilingual education fit comfortably under the Equal Protection Clause paradigm, even though we never really relied upon the U.S. Constitution for our authority since there were more reliable sources. The tension arose because this equal protection argument dissipated when a child became adequately proficient in English, and it did not apply to English-speaking Chicano kids. The equal protection paradigm not only under-girded the courtroom efforts, it was also the least threatening, most understandable argument to state and federal legislators being asked to pass bilingual programs.

Rice and I did massive discovery to establish that Texas had failed LEP children. We also relied upon a fairly incontrovertible and extensive record of discrimination against Chicanos in the schools of the state. We put this together to argue that the failure to establish programs for Chicano students was a continuation of the statewide discriminatory policies. Our proposed remedy: statewide transitional bilingual programming.

It has been argued that a lawyer is best off facing a good attorney on the other side; whatever victory he achieves will have greater validity. While we had vigorous preliminary legal battles with competent and ideologically driven lawyers, the trial was handed to a woman who had some competency issues and little support. Following a month-long trial and considerable post-trial briefing, the court ruled for us completely, ordering a statewide bilingual education remedy.

As in most trials, there were some light moments as well as scary ones. With one prominent linguist, we hit each pole. This particular individual was an internationally known linguist who agreed to appear for us without fee, because he was supportive of what we were doing. Prior to his appointed day in court, we had extended telephone conversations with him, but we were probably soft on him knowing what a jewel we had been handed. He flew into Tyler, Texas, the night before he was to appear—no small feat. At 9:00 p.m., Rice and I started to prepare him to testify the next morning. As the night went on, we became more and more concerned. It was impossible to shake our expert from analogizing bilingual education to a good orgasm: If one language was good, two were *magnífico*. While Judge Justice was politically liberal, he was famous for being straight-laced. This testimony seemed like it could knock us off track. At 2:00 a.m., we informed our expert that his testimony would be redundant. We stated that Judge Justice disliked redundancy, not a total fabrication. The now-released witness respected our judgment, but he indicated that he might still watch the show before he caught his plane. We were greatly concerned as we envisioned having to indicate to the judge that the morning would be slow due to a lack of witnesses, but we had previously listed this expert! We planted people outside the courthouse and at our motel to interdict our expert. Fortunately, he must have woken up and decided to get out as soon as possible. All of our concerns were resolved.

Tyler, where I would soon try *Plyler v. Doe* (1982), had a sympathetic judge but little else. It was close to the Louisiana border, and it was clearly in the Deep South. For the first time, I encountered elderly Black folks who were afraid to look a White person in the eye. One weekend, when Rice and I were stuck in town, we went to breakfast at a coffee shop. While we surely did not look like hippies, we apparently carried an odor that marked us as out-of-towners. When we walked in, several men still in their hunting garb looked us over and commented: "It looks like the Iranians have invaded"—this during the Iranian hostage crisis.

After pondering the evidence for over a year, Judge Justice ruled (*U.S. v. Texas*, 1981). Tying the massive history of discrimination against Chicanos throughout the state to its failure to adequately address the language needs of Texas's LEP students, who were overwhelmingly Chicano, the court ordered the state to enact legislation that would provide a TBE program to all needy kids in Texas.

Judge Justice's ruling shifted the center of action to Austin, the Texas state capital. The judge gave the state legislature several months to come up with a law that met his concerns. We worked closely with several Chicano politicians to fashion a law that would extend bilingual education to all LEP students in the state. Though tricksters in the Office of the Attorney General and in the Texas legislature tried to separate us from our clients, several prominent Texas Chicano organizations, they failed. Texas passed a law that did much of what we wanted, but extended bilingual education only through the sixth grade.[23] The battle shifted back to Tyler, where we challenged the gaps in the law. After hearings, Judge Justice ruled in our favor, holding that the new Texas law had not gone far enough.

While this was going on, Texas State Attorney General Mark White took command of the case away from the attorney who had represented the state at trial. The attorney general sought to disavow the actions and agreements of the trial counsel, demanding a new trial. Things became quite bitter as we felt that many of his claims were fabrications. The judge regularly agreed with us, the law went into effect, and the case moved on to the U.S. Court of Appeals for the Fifth Circuit.

While we all have been exposed to arguments about whether judges are neutral referees or bring their life experiences and inclinations to the process, few practicing lawyers have found pure referees. Judge Justice clearly saw a Texas world that had disadvantaged minority pupils and needed redress. When we saw our three-judge panel in New Orleans, we knew we had gone to the other side. As we predicted going in, the Fifth Circuit ruled that while Judge Justice had ample evidence to rule against Texas on liability, he should have accepted the law passed by the Texas legislature as a remedy. To reach this decision, it was necessary

---

[23] Texas school districts are allowed but not required to offer bilingual education above the elementary level under Texas Education Code §29.0151, Texas Education Agency Regulations §89.1203, 37 Texas Regulation §3822, and 43 Texas Regulation §4731.

for the Court to buy into the attorney general's claim that a rogue attorney had represented Texas at the trial. In one part of the opinion, the Fifth Circuit characterized my filings against White's reformulations of the evidence as "savage attacks." Thus, a *salvaje* was born.

Though we lost the appeal, the law passed by the Texas legislature. This would not have occurred without our U.S. District Court victory, which remained in effect and is still in effect to this day. Though it has not solved all of the learning problems caused by language and poverty, it no doubt has helped numerous children escape from the hopelessness that "sink or swim" had laid upon generations of Texas children.

6

Chicano Desegregation

Throughout my tenure at the Mexican American Legal Defense Fund (MALDEF), I appeared in numerous desegregation cases, mostly in Texas. Chicano communities rarely supported desegregation with the same vigor as in African American circles, but the shenanigans of mostly White school boards in responding to Black-White desegregation orders necessitated a Chicano presence. For example, a number of school districts had no difficulty discerning and discriminating against Chicanos when it served their needs, but these same school districts would ascribe "Whiteness" to Chicanos to meet their integration obligations. By this device, the school districts could minimize the integration of Anglo children. One-way busing, school closures in Chicano neighborhoods, and dispersal of children in need of bilingual education were all threats from White school boards operating under desegregation orders.

The one case initiated by Chicanos in which I was involved was in El Paso. Avila tried the liability phase of this case while I was between jobs at the Center for Law and Education and MALDEF. When I joined MALDEF, the case was turned over to me and Avila moved on to his first love: voting rights litigation.

El Paso Desegregation

Judge William Sessions, who had moved out to El Paso from San Antonio, tried the desegregation case, handing us a split decision (*Alvarado v. El Paso ISD*, 1976). A number of schools, especially those that served the U.S. military base at Fort Bliss, were found to have been intentionally segregated and in need of integration. There was a law that stated that evidence of intentional segregation in one sector set a high bar for the school district to show that segregation in other sectors was free from taint (*Keyes v. School District No. 1*, 1973). But, Judge Sessions minimized the need for integration throughout the El Paso Independent School District. Notably, however, there was an order requiring this high desert school district to assure that predominantly minority schools had air-conditioning.

One issue that arose in the desegregation remedial phase of virtually all cases was the question of whether busing was required at lower grade levels. Whenever the answer was yes, school districts tried to force the burden of busing onto the minority community. This fight occurred in El Paso, and the judge generally supported us. Both sides appealed. The U.S. Court of Appeals for the Fifth Circuit upheld the rulings by Judge Sessions.

During this time, I worked on the *Morales v. Shannon* (1975), *Ross v. Houston Independent School District* (1977), and *U.S. v. Texas Education Agency et al.* (1978) cases in Texas. Austin was notorious for the commitment of the federal judge, Sam Roberts, to the maintenance of the segregated status quo; only after numerous appeals to the Fifth Circuit Court of Appeals was anyone integrated (*U.S. v. Texas Education Agency*, 1978).

Houston Desegregation

The Houston case, *Ross v. Houston Independent School District* (1977), was a particular charmer. The case was started by Thurgood Marshall when he was a young man, and I inherited it at a time when a particularly affluent White area, Westheimer, was to be added to the desegregation plan. This area sought to be excluded from the reach of the law, so we joined the Houston Independent School District (HISD) in opposing this breakaway. While HISD wrapped itself in self-righteousness, its strongest motivation for fighting Westheimer was fear over the loss of taxable wealth. Westheimer was represented by a flamboyant lawyer nicknamed Tex, who wore a particularly large rock on one of his fingers. Tex seemed well on his way to convincing Judge James Noel of the legality of the Westheimer breakaway, when it surfaced that the judge had removed his own child from HISD and placed him in the neighboring Spring Branch Independent School District after an earlier judge had ordered busing in HISD. This occasion resulted in a motion to disqualify Judge Noel.

The motion was greeted by silence; possibly more than 9 months elapsed while the judge pondered whether to disqualify himself. Finally, one afternoon, a call came ordering all counsel to be in the courtroom the following morning for Judge Noel's decision. I flew in from San Francisco, while other lawyers flew in from Washington, New York, and elsewhere. As we sat in the courtroom, the judge began to read his decision, which, if memory serves, exceeded 50 pages. The judge rejected the recusal motion; he claimed he had removed his son from Houston schools to address his son's acne problem, coincidentally on the same day the desegregation was ordered. The judge reasoned that football shoulder pads had been the cause of his son's debilitating problem, and if he were sent to the Spring Branch district his son would have to play basketball instead and the acne problem would disappear. As we filed out of court, a reporter suggested next day's headline should read: "Desegregation Cures Acne."

While Judge Noel refused to recuse himself, Judge Reynaldo Garza of the U.S. Court of Appeals for the Fifth Circuit ordered the case to be transferred within days. For a short while, we had Judge Finis Cowan, a rock-solid judge who was planning to give Westheimer its day in court and render a fair decision. Unfortunately, Judge Cowan decided that he could not afford to maintain his large family on the salary of a federal judge and chose to leave the bench. Judge Robert O'Conor from Laredo was brought in as his replacement. He appointed a flashy Houston lawyer, Joe Jamail, to represent the "children of Houston." Judge O'Conor and Judge Jamail used their court time doing Abbott and Costello routines, rather than adding to the deliberations. Notwithstanding the circus atmosphere, Westheimer was prevented from breaking away. It may have helped that a tax-wealthy section of the city, predominantly housing racial minorities, threatened to initiate its own break off.

Simultaneously, we were denied intervention status in other cases, notably those in Detroit (*Milliken v. Bradley*, 1974) and Milwaukee (*Amos v. Board of School Directors of City of Milwaukee*, 1976). These cases had a long history that preceded our effort, so this result was understandable. Nevertheless, given the propensity of White school boards toward mischief, and the fact that African American representatives had their hands full looking after their own community interests, it is not hard to imagine that Latino children in districts without representation suffered.

Chicago Desegregation

My involvement in Chicago provided me with an image of the brute political forces ruling the city. In its own way, my experience reinforced my perception of a failed political process, and it underscored the need for an independent judiciary whenever race and power are conjoined. Since the early days of integration, there had been efforts by the federal and state government to achieve a level of integration in Chicago with little effect. By the late 1970s, there were still substantial pockets of White children attending virtually all-White public schools in the city. Conversely, segregated Black and Latino schools were also the norm. With great fanfare, a liberal state commissioner of education, supported by the Illinois State Board of Education (ISBE), decided to change this. The mantra proclaimed: Never again will Chicago get away.

The ISBE demanded that Chicago come up with a real desegregation plan. It also asked Professor Gary Orfield, a prominent scholar of desegregation efforts, to convene an expert panel to evaluate this plan. I was asked to be one of the expert panel members, examining it from a Latino perspective. The clear expectation was that the expert panel would be able to quickly dismiss the claims of integration, thereby enabling the ISBE to summon the courage to reject the Chicago plan. This would allow the ISBE to then impose penalties until a real desegregation plan was submitted.

Chicago lived up to expectations. It submitted a desegregation plan that we were asked to evaluate. Over a long weekend, we prepared our analysis. Our conclusion: Little or no integration could be expected under this plan. The analysis was submitted to the ISBE, and a meeting was scheduled in Rockford to determine how to proceed.

Presumably to assist in the rejection of the Chicago desegregation plan and provide proof of our existence, our expert panel joined the ISBE in Rockford. Consideration of the plan moving forward was a two-step process. First, a subcommittee of the ISBE was to consider the submission, our report, and any reply by Chicago. This occurred during the first evening of the board meeting, which I remember included a substantial percentage of the ISBE members. The subcommittee soundly rejected the Chicago submission. Virtually all members, with television cameras whirring, denounced the desegregation plan as a sham. As we went to bed, the expert panelists congratulated themselves on a job well done. The next morning the full board met, again in the glare of publicity, but something had changed. Virtually without exception, the ISBE members, many of whom had expressed disdain for the Chicago desegregation plan the previous evening, heaped praise. When the vote to accept or reject the plan was called, virtually all voted to accept.

What had occurred? During the night, the ISBE members had received a spate of phone calls from representatives of Chicago Mayor Michael Bilandic. As told to us in confidence, all ISBE members had family or friends who worked for the city government. A vote for rejection of the desegregation plan could have jeopardized the livelihoods of their loved ones. The personal trumped the public.

Weeks later, Professor Orfield, a political scientist and no stranger to Chicago, sent me a book, *Don't Make No Waves . . . Don't Back No Losers: An Insider's Analysis of the Daley Machine* (Rakove, 1976). It was a critique of the way Mayor Richard Daley's machine, of which Bilandic was an heir, assured its goals were achieved. The outcome of this fiasco was foretold in the book. While Chicago politics in that era may have been extreme, the lesson is generalizable: The concentration of power is going to thwart the public good when no credible independent checks exist. This is almost preordained when power is held by one racial group—irrespective of the group wielding power.

From Desegregation to Bilingual Education in Denver

As mentioned, the bilingual education initiative of *U.S. v. Texas* (1981) grew out of a statewide desegregation effort, which had prompted bilingual education in a desegregation order of two small school districts in South Texas, San Felipe and Del Rio. In the end, Judge Justice's ruling stood on independent findings of lawfully inadequate responses to the language needs of Texas Chicanos and a generalized pattern of discrimination. Thus, it was not necessary to piggyback on a desegregation order. But, this option still seemed alive after a U.S. Supreme Court ruling in Detroit, which suggested that problems flowing from segregation were fair game in sculpting remedial orders (*Milliken v. Bradley,* 1974). In this first U.S. Supreme Court case addressing segregation issues in the North, the Court ruled that acts that segregated schools afforded the same level of proof of unlawful intent as formal segregation policies typically found in the South. The Court also ruled that a finding of intentional segregation in a significant segment of a school district created the presumption that the entire district was intentionally segregated.

In 1969, African American plaintiffs had filed suit against Denver Public Schools, alleging that they were *intentionally* segregated. When the U.S. Supreme Court remanded the case to a lower court to fashion a remedy, MALDEF was allowed to intervene. The organization relied on Court findings, which suggested that the parallel segregation of Hispanic students in Denver was likely the product of intentionally segregating African American students. The Court acknowledged that Hispanics were seen as a non-White group in the Southwest, and therefore they suffered similarly at the hands of a White power structure.

The intervention on remand was viewed as an opportunity to build upon the victory in San Felipe-Del Rio. Thus, Cárdenas and a colleague presented powerful testimony showcasing how Hispanic/Chicano school failures were caused in major part by cultural incompatibilities between an Anglo-centric system and Chicano children. Language incompatibility was one major barrier to success, they testified. Impressed by the strength of their testimony, the district judge ordered bilingual education in addition to district-wide desegregation. This order was appealed, and the U.S. Court of Appeals for the Tenth Circuit found fault. In short, the Court ruled that segregation alone did not automatically justify a bilingual decree (*Keyes v. School District No. 1*, 1975). From the Court's perspective, the intervenors had to show a legally inadequate response by Denver Public Schools to the language needs of these children in order to secure a sweeping language decree. The Court left open the possibility that the intervenors might go forward to present such evidence.

This is where matters stood upon my arrival at MALDEF in 1976. Early on, the decision was made to meet the challenge presented by the Tenth Circuit Court of Appeals. It took approximately 4 years to amass the evidence needed. Theoretically, Denver had a program to address the needs of limited English speakers. So, we focused our attention on the identification of children in need and the adequacy of the response to their language needs, assuming that the response needed to include a viable program to teach English as well as provide curricular access. Our evidence showed that identification was hit or miss, highly dependent on the whims and prejudices of untrained school employees. As we encountered elsewhere, untrained teachers (and occasionally secretaries) observed a child's modest English production and concluded he did not need special assistance. The school district alleged it delivered a native language bilingual program to some Spanish speakers, but the proof reflected that the education often was left to aides with little more than a high school education. These same aides were often charged with teaching English using a rote method. Non-English speakers rarely received anything more than this abbreviated ESL approach. For most days, children sat in regular classrooms not comprehending the bulk of instruction.

Despite these limitations, the school district attempted to show that it had great success. It could show that children who arrived in a Denver public school with no English could increase their language proficiency quickly. Our rejoinder, which prevailed, was that if you start with no English and you are thrown into an English-only environment, you are bound to improve—to a point. That point was far short of the proficiency needed to succeed in school. Ultimately, the school district could not demonstrate that its program left children with such English proficiency or that children had not suffered a deficit from lack of access.

Judge Richard Matsch, who would subsequently try the Oklahoma City bomber, was an appointee of President Nixon. Nevertheless, he was open and fair. He had also learned something about official doubletalk while presiding over the desegregation case. Almost a year and a half after the last witness took the stand, he ruled that the Denver schools had failed limited English-speaking children (*Keyes v. School District No. 1*, 1983).

Typically, institutional reform via civil rights cases involves a two-step process. First, the plaintiffs must establish liability. If they succeed, the case moves to a second phase in which the defendant must come forward with a corrective plan. Ordinarily, plaintiffs challenge the adequacy of the defendant's response. In the end, the judge is left to choose between the parties, sometimes taking pieces from each side as part of the final order.

I chose to approach this remedial phase differently. If we could develop a remedial plan jointly with the school district, I thought the likelihood of buy-in would be greater. Ultimately, implementation of remedies is left to those who messed up in the first place and oversight is usually imperfect. Also, if the defendants in these cases are willing to earnestly engage in developing a remedy, they can provide insights and expertise that outside litigators may lack. The upshot of this approach was an extensive plan that addressed each of the areas the court had found fault with.

It had become clear from other cases that native language instruction was not legally required; however, the Court had ruled that this was an acceptable response to assure curricular access when properly implemented (*Keyes v. School District No. 1*, 1983). Thus, the negotiated plan relied heavily on bilingual instruction for Spanish speakers. It also established programs to ensure that teachers were appropriately trained and linguistically skilled to serve the needs of these children.

Although MALDEF represented the needs of Mexican American children, our class included limited English speakers of other languages as well. Most of these non-Spanish speakers were of Hmong heritage; these children had landed in Denver in the aftermath of the Vietnam War. While provision of Hmong bilingual education was not logistically possible, we did build in orders for hiring Hmong aides who could act as liaisons with parents and creating an Asian advisory group to serve as a pressure group for the interest of Hmong children; finally, we asked for heightened ESL services. Ironically, soon after the order was entered, the majority of these families left Denver for Fresno, California, following a religious leader.

This experience allowed us to gain illuminating insights about the choice and use of experts. By the time we got to Denver, Rice and I had developed a reputation that enabled us to enlist a prestigious array of experts: Arthur Flemming, chairman of the U.S. Commission on Civil Rights; Courtney Cazden, a distinguished faculty member at the Harvard Graduate School of Education; and, Kenji Hakuta, an up-and-coming scholar at Yale University. These were among the talented and committed witnesses we presented; clearly, a court has to take these kinds of people seriously. Throwing their reputation behind your assertions gives your case a gravitas that less prestigious experts are unable to add. However, it is crucial that you do not rest on their reputations. Furthermore, your experts must understand the court setting, and they must learn to explain abstract theories using examples. This allows a judge, who does not share their expertise, to make sense of the information offered.

Generally, our experts performed admirably in Denver, but we did have one close call—probably the result of not following the above admonitions. One expert (none of the above) decided to enlist the judge in an exercise, which no doubt worked well with his students. It involved the witness speaking gibberish and then asking the judge to state his understanding of what was said. This was to show the discomfort of a non-English speaker in an English-only classroom. However, this violated a central thesis of trial practice: Don't make the judge look like a fool. In any event, Judge Matsch took it in good humor, and no harm was done.

7

The Right of Undocumented Students to Schooling: *Plyler v. Doe*

Certainly, the most significant engagement of my career was the case known as *Plyler v. Doe* (1982). In 1976, the state of Texas passed legislation that effectively excluded undocumented children from its schools. While not a direct prohibition, the law withheld state funds from school districts for undocumented children. In response, school districts either excluded these children or charged tuition to compensate for the lost state revenue. Needless to say, charging tuition was tantamount to exclusion for the vast majority of these low-income children.

I became engaged in the problem soon after arriving at the Mexican American Legal Defense Fund (MALDEF). Cárdenas had asked me to meet with Chicano superintendents in the Rio Grande Valley to convince them that they should continue to admit undocumented students; they could do so, albeit without state reimbursement. Even though there was sympathy for this position, our efforts failed. The issue was that there had been a substantial influx of recent immigrants from neighboring Mexican states, and there was no room to house these students. As our trial judge, Judge Justice, observed, this was a problem of the state's own making, and one which the U.S. Supreme Court had failed to relieve in *San Antonio Independent School District v. Rodríguez* (1973). These poor school districts, highly dependent on an impoverished local tax base, could not generate enough money to

Left to right: Peter Roos, Tom Saenz, Vilma Martínez, and Michael Olivas
at a conference commemorating the *Plyler v. Doe* case in 2017.
Reprinted with permission from the University of Houston.

adequately educate its long-term residents, much less the influx of new students.

While these factors immobilized sympathetic super-intendents, the passage of the law was primarily the product of xenophobia that periodically strikes the American populace. Major support for the legislation came from legislators far removed from the problems of the border. I waited for what I considered to be a good opportunity to challenge the law. In the meantime, a challenge brought through the state courts of Texas in *Hernandez v. Houston Independent School District* (1977) was lost.

Just before Labor Day in 1977, an opportunity presented itself. A call came into MALDEF's San Francisco office from a civil rights attorney, Larry Daves in Tyler, Texas. An employee of the local Catholic school had contacted Daves to ask what could be done about the forthcoming exclusion of undocumented children from the Tyler Independent School District. The Catholic school had tried to accommodate these children, but the burden was too much. The Tyler school district had educated these children on its own dime for several years before reluctantly deciding that it could no longer do so. Within 24 hours of the call from Daves, I was on a plane to Tyler, a modest-sized town in East Texas known (at least to itself) as the rose capital of the world. In fact, many of the parents of these excluded children had been drawn there to work in the rose fields.

I was drawn to this case by several factors. First, there was a committed local counsel. Second, Judge Justice sat in Tyler. While it was clear that this case would be decided by an appellate court, having an understanding judge was important, because we certainly would have no problem presenting our evidence. This increased likelihood of an early victory was attractive. Finally, Tyler was far removed from the border, and it had relatively few undocumented students.

School was scheduled to open the following Tuesday, so we felt the need to be in court that morning to request a temporary injunction against the school district. In oppressive heat, which had been the norm all summer, we worked around the clock to have our papers ready for the judge. Daves, Bobbie Rodkin, a young lawyer in his office, and I trooped into the judge's chambers after giving notice to school district's counsel. To our surprise, the judge refused to grant us the temporary relief we sought. Instead, he proceeded on several fronts. First, he picked up the phone and called the state attorney general and the U.S. Department of Justice to inform them about our filing. While his call to the Texas state capitol in Austin likely followed ours, no one from the Office of the Attorney General had appeared. His calls were based on the recognition that our filing had both state and national implications. Second, the judge issued an order on our request against the defendants and their counsel from disclosing the identity of the undocumented plaintiffs. We had been very concerned that exposing the identities of the plaintiffs would put them at risk. Finally, the court set a hearing for a preliminary injunction—which ordinarily would stay in effect much longer than the temporary restraining order we were seeking—for the following Friday.

Recognizing that we would have to present the parents of excluded students at the hearing, we requested that the hearing occur in camera or out of public view. We viewed this as a necessary extension of the protective order mentioned above. To this latter request, the judge balked, holding that a public hearing could only be dispensed with when there were national security concerns. To balance our concern that parents would not and could not risk exposure at a public hearing, the judge did a curious thing. He set the hearing for 6:00 a.m., believing that no one would get up that early to attend the hearing. It turned out he was right.

For the next 3 days, we honed our case at the Tyler Holiday Inn. Though Tyler was located in a "dry" county, our evenings were spent in the hotel bar, a members-only establishment. A stagecoach in the middle of the bar served as the home of a disc jockey whose favorite song was *Up Against the Wall Redneck Mother* (Hubbard, 1973). When we felt like spoiling ourselves, we headed to the best restaurant in town. It was an Italian eatery, which featured a "wop" salad on the menu; political correctness was in short supply in East Texas during 1977.

At 5:30 a.m. that Friday, we hauled our clients and materials through the dark cobblestone streets to the courthouse. We were met by bailiffs who were less than pleased to find themselves at work at that hour. Our clients were escorted to an area below the courtroom, while we reviewed our request to protect them. The Court was adamant that the impending hearing be open to the public, and it further refused to extend the protective order to the U.S. Department of Justice. In short, by testifying, the parents would be exposing themselves to federal officials who could hasten their deportation. It was the Court's view that it could not do anything to restrict the federal government from executing its responsibilities. Despite all this, Michael Weiss, the young U.S. Department of Justice lawyer, informed the Court and ourselves that the government had no intention of retaliating against the parents.

We descended to the holding area below the court to inform the parents of the limits of the protections we were able to secure and to give them the choice to go forward or not. The case sat in

the balance. Without exception, the parents decided to go forward. To them, the education of their children came before any risk—a risk they had taken in part to assure a better life for their children. The parents testified. All were hard-working individuals who had taxes withheld from paychecks, who paid property taxes as renters and sales taxes as consumers. None had received any public aid, and their children had been brought to the country not of their individual choice but by their parents who were committed to keeping their families together.

The only hitch in the testimony of the parents was interpretation. There were no formal interpreters in Tyler in the late 1970s. Thus, we enlisted Mr. McAndrew, who had brought the case to the Daves office, to serve in this capacity. Meanwhile, a high school Spanish teacher assisted counsel with interpretation for the Tyler ISD. This teacher took his job seriously, regularly stating his objection to interpretation by McAndrew. We therefore decided things would go more smoothly if this teacher became the "official" interpreter, and so he replaced McAndrew. This teacher interpreter was a godsend, smoothing over all rough patches of our clients' testimony. Following testimony and presentation of written and oral arguments, the Court granted the preliminary injunction. Thus, until trial, which was set for December, all undocumented students in Tyler were to be admitted to school.

The trial took place over 3 or 4 days in December of 1977. A central issue was whether undocumented children were taking scarce resources away from citizens. The legal counterpart to this issue was whether there was a rational or compelling reason for preferring one group of innocent kids over another just to save money. The law seemed to say that saving money alone could not support such a distinction. In fact, we were able to show that undocumented status had nothing to do with cost. Despite common conceptions, undocumented children were not appreciably more likely to have costly language or educational needs merely because of birth across a border. Some low-income citizens and some undocumented children had unusual educational needs, but many did not.

The Supreme Court in 1982, at the time of *Plyler v Doe*, posing with
President Reagan in the Supreme Court Conference Room. From left to right:
Justice Harry Blackmun, Justice Thurgood Marshall, Justice William Brennan,
Chief Justice Warren Burger, President Reagan, Justice Sandra Day O'Connor,
Justice Byron White, Justice Lewis F. Powell, Jr., Justice William Rehnquist and
Justice John Paul Stevens. Photo: Ronald Reagan Library.

Many factors contribute to educational need. Immigration
status, by itself, is irrelevant. The term "undocumented" applies
not just to recent arrivals, but to many children who have been in
the United States virtually their entire lives. The state presented a
study regarding the needs of immigrant students, which could not
differentiate between those with lawful and those with "unlawful" status. Indeed, we were able to show that the exclusion of
undocumented students resulted in reduction of resources for
citizen children who remained in school districts like those in
Tyler, given the way Texas law worked.

In cases with such a broad public policy sweep, it is usually
necessary to bust common misconceptions, even those that have
only modest legal relevance. Thus, we were able to show through
experts that the number of undocumented students in Texas was
still a small percentage of the overall school population. Further,
we were able to show that employment, not education, was the
principal draw to America, and that U.S. policy in many ways
encouraged undocumented immigration to meet labor needs.

In the end, as the decision reflects, Judge Justice ruled in *Doe v. Plyler* (1978) that the denial of education to innocent children in Tyler, and by extension Texas, denied them equal protection under the law. He also concluded that whatever problems existed in the Rio Grande Valley were primarily the result of the state's school finance scheme. While the U.S. Supreme Court had refused to strike down that system in *San Antonio Independent School District v. Rodríguez* (1973), it had criticized the scheme as reflecting a questionable choice, thus providing additional fodder for Judge Justice's decision.

The Filing of *In Re Alien Children*

When we filed *Plyler v. Doe* (1978), I made a snap decision to limit our class of plaintiffs to Tyler, even though the case was a challenge to Texas state law. This decision was made with two thoughts in mind: First, it was feared that if we sought to certify a statewide class, complications would ensue that might slow down or damage the interests of our *Plyler* (1978) parents who had put so much on the line. Second, it seemed clear that the case would ultimately be decided by an appellate court and thus benefit all undocumented students in Texas. It also seemed likely there would be a fair opportunity to expedite an appeal.

The *Plyler v. Doe* (1978) decision exerted pressure to obtain relief for the remainder of Texas's undocumented students. Soon after our district court decision was announced, several piggyback cases were consolidated in Houston by several legal aid attorneys supported by Peter Schey, an immigration and civil rights attorney in Los Angeles. Building upon the evidence we had presented in Tyler, *In Re Alien Children* (1980), a case that was more vigorously fought by the state, the plaintiffs again prevailed. *In Re Alien Children* (1980) extended the *Plyler v. Doe* (1978) ruling statewide at the same time that we were preparing for the appellate argument. The state sought a stay of *In Re Alien Children* (1980) from the Supreme Court of Texas. Denying a broad stay, Justice Lewis Powell granted individual school districts the right to seek a stay if they could establish that they would suffer irreparable harm if forced to implement the ruling (*Certain Named and Unnamed Non-Citizen Children v. Texas*, 1980).

A Joyous Day in Brownsville

The Brownsville Independent School District, just across the border from Matamoros, Mexico, applied for a stay, which was assigned to Judge Ballesteros, a member of an old Brownsville family. The judge granted a temporary stay allowing the district to exclude undocumented students pending a further hearing. When the temporary stay was issued, Schey responded with a highly inflammatory blast against the judge. When the dust settled, he recognized that he was not the ideal choice to appear at the hearing to extend the stay through the appellate process. As such, I was asked to take the lead with Linda Yañez, a local legal aid attorney.

While preparing for the hearing that morning, I was handed a note from Judge Jimmy DeAnda, who had recently joined the federal bench. I knew Judge DeAnda as a MALDEF board member. More importantly, I knew him as the fearless advocate for Chicano civil rights who had argued one of the most significant Chicano cases to go before the U.S. Supreme Court. *Hernandez v. Texas* (1954), decided on the same day as *Brown v. Board of Education of Topeka* (1954), had ruled unconstitutional the practice of excluding Chicanos from grand juries. DeAnda's note asked me to come up to his chambers in the courthouse following the conclusion of our hearing before Judge Ballesteros.

As we settled into our seats in preparation for the first witness, the judge entered the courtroom and announced that the hearing would not go forward. The U.S. Court of Appeals for the Fifth Circuit had unanimously ruled that we had prevailed in *Plyler v. Doe* (1980). With this decision, the hearing had become moot. I floated as in a dream up to Judge DeAnda's chambers. On entry, I found not only DeAnda, but U.S. Circuit Judge Garza, a veteran of the historic battles for equality for Chicanos in Texas.

Abrazos and congratulations rained on me from the two individuals who had done probably the most in the courts to fight for Chicano rights; little could have been better. That night, David Hall, a legendary legal aid leader in South Texas, and I hit a good number of bars in Matamoros. Drowning our Cabrito tequila with Negra Modelo beers, the coming preparation for the inevitable appeal to the U.S. Supreme Court was forgotten.

In keeping with the imprint of legendary civil rights figures on *Plyler v. Doe* (1980), the Fifth Circuit ruling had been written by Judge Frank Johnson, an Alabama district court judge, sitting by designation. Judge Johnson, like Judge Justice, no doubt lived with an entourage of body guards as a result of his commitment to the Fourteenth Amendment of the U.S. Constitution. He had ordered a number of Alabama school districts to desegregate, and he had also ordered the reformation of Alabama's notorious prisons. He had not been part of the panel initially announced to hear the case, but he magically appeared when the three-judge panel entered the court to hear the argument.

Though the U.S. Supreme Court was not compelled to accept the case, no one was surprised when it did so. In addition to accepting *Plyler v. Doe* (1982) for argument, the Court joined *In Re Alien Children* (1980). Though Schey had a reputation in some quarters for self-promotion, we were able to work fairly harmoniously. His expertise with immigration issues and my background in education helped create a division of labor that minimized conflict.

In preparing the briefs and argument, I was reminded once again of the pressures, either unique or accentuated, in appearing before the U.S. Supreme Court. The Court's role as the final arbiter of issues with important public policy implications requires the advocate to deeply consider the national, occasionally international, implications of his positions. Pure precedent can never provide all the answers, as is often the case at lower levels.

Plyler v. Doe (1982) had a plethora of issues that had to be sensitively addressed. First, a number of well-meaning advocates would have liked the case to serve as a declaration that undocumented individuals constituted a suspect class. If the Court were to so rule, any denial of benefits or welfare could be credibly questioned. However, I determined that if the Court felt it had to make such a ruling to support my position, then we would certainly lose the case. Conversely, there were those who wished to emphasize that this law excluding undocumented individuals from public schools was merely a continuation of racial discrimination, which was legally suspect given Texas's past. Though we had presented some of this information at trial, I thought that a decision too reliant on history could effectively only cover Texas. There was also a group of lawyers who saw this case as a vehicle for greater reliance by the Court on international human rights law. In their view, the U.S. court system gave insufficient value to expressions of concern for such things as the right to education expressed in international protocols. I urged them to file an amicus brief arguing their point of view. Given the U.S. Supreme Court's limited attraction to international expressions of rights, I refused to use my limited briefing time or presentation to advance this admirable goal. Finally, the U.S. Supreme Court in the *San Antonio Independent School District v. Rodríguez* (1973) school finance case had ruled that education was not a fundamental interest, and some saw *Plyler v. Doe* (1982) as an opportunity to revisit that recent decision.

In the end, I chose to not force a ruling based on any one of these factors. If you added up the racial undertones of the political powerlessness of the class of undocumented persons and combined this with the fact that a total denial of education might not invite strict scrutiny but would require some heightened concern, it seemed to me the Court would find a way to rule in our favor. The upshot would be a victory and, equally as important, avoiding a loss, which no doubt would prompt schooling denials of undocumented students nationally. While the downside of this additive approach would make our victory less of a precedent for other cases, our obligation to secure a meaningful educational victory for undocumented students seemed paramount.

Some words about preparation for oral argument: While it is comfortable to plan an oral argument by honing your affirmative case, a U.S. Supreme Court argument is usually more about explaining away apparent or real weaknesses. Thus, I imagined every possible hostile question I could, and I developed clear and concise rejoinders to each. If I waivered on my responses, it would show a lack of confidence in their veracity. Thus, as I had done in *Goss v. López* (1975), I spent the last several days before the argument walking the streets of Washington, DC., speaking out of both sides of my mouth: "Mr. Roos, how do you explain...?" "Your honor...!" Never did I receive a question or follow-up question that I was not fully and quickly prepared for. While there may be some who denigrate oral argument, it seems to me that confident and rational responses to perceived weaknesses in argument can win the day in a close case.

At oral argument, another slippery-slope question presented itself. At one point, I was asked whether this case would open up a right to higher education for undocumented students. Our fear was that the Court would deny *all* schooling to undocumented children if it thought it had to rule beyond elementary and secondary schooling; or, alternatively, we feared that the Court would expressly preclude postsecondary schooling, a highly undesirable result. My response to this question, which appeared to calm the waters, was to ask the Court to punt. I emphasized the fact that the students before the Court in this case were minors who had no say in whether to be in the country or not. The Court's decision to avoid a ruling on postsecondary education left enough wiggle room to assist the *Plyler v. Doe* (1982) children as they matured. Indeed, one of my early cases after returning from a sabbatical following the victory on this case involved the rights of undocumented youth; these rights have continued to be litigated up to my retirement.

While *Plyler v. Doe* (1982) has been as definitive as any institutional reform case could be, there have been efforts to circumvent its mandate that undocumented students have a right to elementary and secondary education. The requirement that a student show a Social Security card while enrolling, rationalized as merely an administrative way to keep track of students, has been widely tried and rejected; in fact, the federal government expressly bans the use of a Social Security card as a prerequisite for admission to public schools. Some school districts and states have sought to ask about immigration status for educational planning reasons. These efforts have similarly been struck down. Others have attempted to confound district residency, which is justifiable, with legal residency in the country, but the *Plyler v. Doe* (1982) decision itself addresses this dodge. And, some have seen a vulnerability in the decision, because it was decided by a 5-4 vote. While that might send shivers through the faint of heart, I am convinced that no judge would want to be the fifth vote relegating a huge class of innocent children to a life of serfdom while leaving such an uneducated class to roam the streets of America, unemployed and unemployable. Hopefully, we will not have to test this thesis.

Trying to Create a National Bilingual Mandate

One final set of initiatives from my time at MALDEF deserves mention—efforts to establish a national bilingual mandate. The first of these initiatives included an attempt to administratively create a nationwide right to bilingual and native language education in schools. We came tantalizing close, but we were probably attempting something that was never in the cards for us.

Viewed from the vantage point of 1980, it seemed like a doable, albeit formidable task to have the newly created U.S. Department of Education (ED) require school districts to offer transitional bilingual education. In fact, the ED had already gone down that path through its Office for Civil Rights (OCR). As discussed previously, the OCR had convened a panel following the *Lau v. Nichols* ruling in 1974, which recommended that native language remedies be offered for school districts out of compliance with the Lau Remedies.[24]

In 1978, after the election of President Jimmy Carter, the OCR became more aggressive in combating "sink or swim" approaches used in many states and school districts throughout the country. By 1980, approximately 500 jurisdictions had signed agreements to follow the Lau Remedies. It helped that the newly created ED was headed by Shirley Hufstedler, a previous appellate court judge who had supported the plaintiffs in *Lau v. Nichols* (1974).

While matters were tilting towards a native language and bilingual direction, it seemed to us that the ambiguity between having an upfront mandate and a remedial mandate could be hurtful. It hurt our litigation, which could not rely on the Lau Remedies as a standard for the courts to find liability. It also enabled states and school districts to wait out findings of liability by the OCR before they implemented a bilingual program. Additionally, we felt that when political administrations changed, a bilingual mandate might be harder to accomplish. Thus, we initiated a lobbying effort to turn the Lau Remedies into a standard, along with our improvements.

We had both sympathetic advocates as well as skeptics. Cindy Brown, the director of the OCR, and Josúe González, director of the office that oversaw the federal grant program to assist schools with ELs, were friends who shared our goals. At times, they worked with us to overcome skeptics in the ED led by Undersecretary of Education Mike Smith. Ironically, after leaving office, Smith served on the Multicultural Education, Training and Advocacy (META) board for several years.

---

[24] The Lau Remedies provided a comprehensive analysis for evaluating the adequacy of a school district's response to English learner students. By the terms of the ED, it was not to be utilized unless a school district was out of compliance with *Lau v. Nichols* (1974). Thus, though the Lau Remedies required native language instruction for at least elementary students, it could not be invoked unless there was a lack of a legally acceptable program, which could rely on English as a second language.

After a year of tug-of-war, a draft rule about bilingual education saw the light of day. The public response was instant and hostile. While there were dissenters, much of the media saw this initiative as the heavy hand of the ED. This fed into fears expressed by conservatives that the creation of the new department would lead to a federal takeover of education. The xenophobic voice that had supported limited schooling for undocumented students also weighed in.

Despite the clamor, the rule-making process proceeded. Hearings occurred throughout the country. Rice and I did what we could to enable the voices of those most affected to be heard. Based on the transcripts, we won hands down. But, among the broader public, nothing changed. The ED received massive correspondence hostile to the proposed bilingual rule. In the end, little of this mattered. In 1982, President Ronald Reagan swept into power. Within days, the bilingual regulations were withdrawn.

So, what were the lessons? First, I believe it is always beneficial to explore different venues to accomplish your goals. Often bureaucracies have a liberal bent that can be exploited to achieve liberal goals, such as the institutionalization of bilingual instruction. The flip side? When dealing with interests that are perceived as uniquely associated with a minority group, one should be prepared for a sleeping giant to raise its head. One should never go into battle with the belief that simply because your cause is just to you it will be perceived as just to a majority—or to any one that has not shared the experiences of the minority group you are representing. Finally, there are times when the wisest course is to let progress proceed organically and not to push for too much too soon. This requires a sensitive balancing. It is easy to look at a number of initiatives from desegregation to bilingual education where one could argue that pushing too hard led to a backlash that was harsher than if progress had been allowed to happen. On the other hand, without the push of advocates, it is possible that progress would have been too humble to measure. In any event, consideration of this dynamic is important for advocates.

The NABE Washington Presence

Our second initiative of that era was the placement of a bilingual lobbyist in Washington, DC. While working at MALDEF, I found myself regularly flying there to support funding for the federal bilingual grant program (then Title VII, now Title III), or I was working with the Department of Health, Education, and Welfare, which became the ED. While I could develop relationships with the key players, I was starting to realize that my efforts with the U.S. Congress were abysmal. This represented a serious issue in the late 1970s; MALDEF was really the only Latino organization with a meaningful presence in Washington.[25]

Following the failure to secure the bilingual regulation, several of us convened a meeting of advocates from around the country to assess the damage and to plot a response. Out of this meeting, it was decided that a Washington lobbyist was needed. There was a national organization, the National Association for Bilingual Education (NABE), which theoretically could have picked up the slack, but it was not ready for this sort of commitment. Once again, the responsibility fell on MALDEF. It was the only organization with a nationwide reach and resources to coordinate the effort. Susana Navarro, a young education PhD from Stanford, joined us in trying to bring this vision to fruition. Recognizing that it would take time to hire a lobbyist, we first decided to create a Washington presence with smoke and mirrors. Like a phoenix, the American Coalition for Bilingual Education was created. We opened a P.O. box in the district, which was our "office." We then proceeded to interview potential lobbyists.

Ultimately, we settled on Jim Lyons, who had just left the OCR at the ED. He knew the issues, had time on his hands, and was the cheapest alternative. Even with this low-cost option, though, we had to engage in creative funding. One month we raised his salary by borrowing from a Mexican wedding ritual. People pinned money on Lorenza Calvillo Schmidt, a California

---

[25] This changed in subsequent decades as the National Council of La Raza (NCLR) emerged as a powerhouse.

State Board of Education member, and me as they came up to dance with us at an awards ceremony in Los Angeles. Ultimately, we convinced NABE to hire Lyons. He remained there for 15 or more years, and he was a balance against the constant assaults on bilingual education in our nation's capital. He also became the staff of the organization, helping it to professionalize. Ultimately, as these things happen, Lyons got caught up in NABE intrigue and lost his job.

Meanwhile, on June 15, 1982, the stars aligned. It was my wife Emma's birthday and my last day on the job at MALDEF when the U.S. Supreme Court ruled in *Plyler v. Doe* (1982). On the day following the ruling, Larry Daves's office in Tyler was inundated by roses, a lovely thank you from parents who picked roses in the fields and whose children now had access to public schools. My going-away party at Lake Temescal in Oakland was particularly sweet, as was a gathering arranged by the Chicano Education Project led by Federico Peña outside of Denver, which I attended as I worked my way to Madrid for a much-needed break and semisuccessful effort to learn Spanish.

In a pattern we would follow until the end of my career, Emma and I periodically spent the better part of a year abroad. Emma met me in Madrid where we bought the smallest, cheapest used Volvo known to man. After traveling through Spain with a teenaged niece from Los Angeles who scandalized everyone except teen boys with her mini-skirts, we settled in London. I had been offered a position as an honorary associate at the Institute of Education at the University of London. While I was not honored by the small honorarium I received, it did give me a great base to observe and learn about English education with an emphasis on programs for immigrants. Interestingly, I had been preceded by David Kirp, who had also preceded me at Harvard's Center for Law and Education. As I remember, Kirp had written an article or book in which he had lauded the English for addressing minority social problems by doing nothing. I was prompted to write a monograph, which documented the legal efforts to address educational discrimination in America (Roos, 1984). I also took modest aim at the claim often advanced in the U.K. that, given the absence of a written constitution, similar litigation was not feasible. Based on other litigation that was ongoing in the U.K., it seemed to me that opportunities existed for advocates and lawyers to address problems that closely resembled those in the U.S.

After a quarter in London, we drove to Greece, sold our car, and took cheap flights to different countries in Asia. One thing I learned through this trip was the value of taking extended breaks after you have worked long and hard. I attribute the ability to continue a vigorous pace until I retired, in part, to the breaks we were able to take every 5 or 6 years. I was able to relight just when burnout was taking hold. After the better part of a year, Emma and I returned to America.

8

The META Years

n my absence, Rice and Camilo Pérez, a young colleague at Harvard's Center for Law and Education (CLE), had secured a grant from the Carnegie Corporation of New York to continue our work with immigrant students. They created a new entity: Multicultural Education, Training and Advocacy (META). Initially, they worked under the umbrella of Harvard's CLE, but soon they struck out on their own. This separation was effectively compelled by the restrictions the U.S. Congress imposed on federally funded legal services.

Compelling California to Monitor School Districts:
Comité de Padres de Familia v. Riles

On my return, I joined META as co-director with Rice. Our initial docket included cases that I had worked on at the Mexican American Legal Defense Fund (MALDEF) that called for a continuity of counsel. I completed the remedial negotiations in Denver, and we moved the *Comité de Padres de Familia v. Riles* (1979) case to fruition, which built on a case I had won at MALDEF, *Idaho Migrant Council v. Board of Education* (1981). That appellate case had established an obligation of states to ensure that school districts were providing legally adequate service to English learner students.

Stefan Rosenzweig, who had left Harvard's CLE, returned to California. Together, we sued the California Department of Education. We alleged that its oversight and enforcement efforts failed to meet the obligations required by *Idaho Migrant Council v. Board of Education* (1981) and *U.S. v. Texas* (1981). After intensive

With Stefan Rosenzweig, late 1990s.

pretrial discovery and extended negotiations, we entered into a settlement that became a consent decree. *Comité de Padres de Familia v. Riles* (1979) required the California Department of Education to collect data annually and to use an agreed-upon format for analysis. In addition, the state was required to go on site to school districts every 3 years and to investigate complaints. Triggers were established to impose penalties on school districts violating the rights of California's English learner students.

In many ways, *Comité de Padres de Familia v. Riles* (1979) provided the legal underpinning for bilingual education in California for the ensuing 15 years. It became particularly important when the Bilingual Education Act was allowed to sunset in 1986. Despite that sunset and with the help of sympathetic state department bureaucrats, California hardly missed a beat until the passage of Proposition 227 in 1997.

Higher Education Access for Undocumented Students: *Leticia A. v. Board of Regents*

It was not long before the question left hanging from the *Plyler v. Doe* (1982) argument surfaced. In California, as in virtually all states, an undocumented student was treated as a nonresident for purposes of tuition. The effect was to require these students to pay a tuition that was many times higher than that paid by all other students who lived in the state. Coupled with the fact that undocumented students were ineligible for any state or federal grants or loans, this was a mirror image of the *Plyler v. Doe* (1982) situation at the postsecondary level. Stated simply, children who may have spent virtually their entire lives in California were barred from attending the state's colleges and universities.

The efforts to challenge this policy had a personal twist—multiplied by two. First, a nephew, Norberto, was admitted to the University of California, Los Angeles (UCLA). Norberto had been brought to California before his first birthday, and he had never been out of the state. In fact, his mother had sent him to Emma for safekeeping while she disentangled herself from an abusive relationship in Mexico. Norberto's mother worked hard, paid taxes, and sent him to a Catholic high school to maximize his obvious abilities. It was only when he applied to UCLA that he discovered that he was undocumented. In every way measurable, other than his immigration status, he was a model 18-year-old. Although Norberto was admitted to UCLA, his mother decided to send him to community college, because it was affordable; UCLA, charging out-of-state tuition, was not. Ultimately, the family chipped in, and Norberto enrolled at UCLA. But, it was unclear whether the funds could last him through graduation. The second personal twist came when my wife, Emma, a bilingual teacher and a vigorous cheerleader for Latino students, invited two sisters to live in our basement after they found out they had been admitted to the University of California, Berkeley. We lived near the campus, and this would assist with the cost. At this point, we learned that they were agonizing over whether to admit they lacked papers, which almost certainly would have put the college beyond their reach. One sister, Leticia, became the lead plaintiff in our challenge to this policy.

In 1985, *Leticia A. v. Board of Regents of the University of California* was filed against the University of California and the California State University system. Robert Rubin, of the Lawyers Committee for Civil Rights and Urban Affairs, joined me as lead counsel. MALDEF was also on the pleadings. The trial in the Superior Court of Alameda County presented a group of students with profiles similar to that of Norberto. We found that students like this were not hard to find, as first-generation immigrants, almost unfailingly, pushed their children to succeed to overcome problems of poverty. "Leticia A." clubs sprang up at a number of schools. Evidence was presented about the potential contributions these students were likely to make if they could maximize their education; this was contrasted with the modest role that they would likely play if denied higher education. Indeed, pathologies lending to prison and becoming a public charge were more likely if their quest for schooling was thwarted. Evidence we presented also showed that these conditions would likely be passed on to offspring.

When the judge ruled that the Constitution of California was violated by this policy, it was before a busload of students who had trekked up from Southern California. By a happy coincidence, which ultimately created problems, the chair of the board of regents of the University of California was the former president and general counsel of MALDEF, Vilma Martínez. Under Martínez's leadership, the University of California decided not to appeal the trial court ruling. Similarly, the California State Universities and community colleges also agreed to accept the ruling. Norberto, Leticia, and many other young Californians were allowed to attend college at tuition identical to their citizen classmates. Of course, their poverty and their inability to access state and federal monies made it considerably more difficult. But, one hurdle had been breached in California.

Several years later, a letter arrived in my inbox. It was from a crank that had sent the same letter to everyone down to me. Sent by an admissions bureaucrat at UCLA, a fellow by the name of Bradford, the letter complained of his obligation to treat undocumented applicants like citizens. It was the sort of letter most of us send to the circular file, which is what I did. After some time, we received a call from an attorney representing the University of California. We were asked: Would you assist with a brief to the

California Court of Appeal? Bradford had filed a challenge to *Leticia A. v. Board of Regents* (1985) through a conservative legal organization. The University of California counsel had failed to notify us of its filing, and thus we had not participated in the trial court where they had lost. Because *Leticia A. v. Board of Regents* (1985) had not been appealed, no binding precedent had been created. The appeals court upheld the trial court, thus vitiating our victory in *Leticia A. v. Board of Regents* (1985).

Legislating Higher Education Access for Undocumented Students: AB 540

Rubin and I made the decision to try our hand at reversing the legislation rather than continuing with the court challenge. We discovered that California had a long history of granting exemptions to its residency laws; a typical exemption was granted to children of police officers killed in the line of duty. The exemption route was attractive, because federal law had made it questionable for a state to directly grant residency to undocumented students.

In drafting the legislation, we reasoned that the closer we could make the beneficiaries of an exemption look like *Plyler v. Doe* (1982) students, the better. Thus, our initial legislation granted an exemption to a student who been brought to the U.S. as a minor, had attended several years of high school in California, and had graduated from a California high school. Richard Polanco agreed to carry our legislation. At the time, he was one of the more powerful members of the California legislature and a great author. As in the litigation, the kids who would be the beneficiaries of the bill were the true salespersons. Their stories were so compelling, and the state benefit in educating them so obvious, that the legislation moved forward with modest opposition. The only blip was a demand by some that the kids would have to agree to apply for a change in immigration status in order to avail themselves of the bill. Since approaching immigration services was so fraught for these kids, we reasoned that this would be a poison pill. We ultimately decided to amend the bill so as to require that the beneficiaries of the exemption just needed to agree to apply for a change of immigration status when eligible.

The bill landed on the desk of Gray Davis, the Democratic governor of California. The governor raised questions about conflicts with federal law, which were answered by the appropriate state lawyers. They agreed with us that granting an exemption from a residency fee coupled with an acknowledgment that undocumented students were beneficiaries provided a shield against applicable federal law. Governor Davis then consulted with his political handlers, who advised against signing the bill. This is all it took for Governor Davis to refuse to sign the bill. After receiving the support of a bipartisan legislature, we ran into a Democratic governor who squashed our efforts. Soon thereafter, Rick Perry, conservative governor of Texas—from the state that had brought us *Plyler v. Doe* (1982)—approved a similar bill.

During the next election cycle, Marco Firebaugh, who had been an aide to Polanco as we pushed through the legislation, was elected to the California State Assembly. In one of his first steps, he proposed that we reintroduce the legislation. With his energy and commitment, the bill again made it through the legislature. This time the governor signed the bill, AB 540.[26]

Although one often looks with despair at racial progress, the education of undocumented students provides evidence that resiliency has its reward. In the early 1980s, we faced the prospect that undocumented students would be denied all education, but by the early 21st century, a number of states followed the Texas and California examples, granting in-state tuition to deserving students regardless of immigration status.

As discussed later, there have been some predictable challenges to these efforts. To date, all have failed. Further, in California, eligible undocumented students can receive state financial aid to supplement in-state fees. All is far from perfect, but those with a dream, a willingness to work, and a just cause can accomplish important work.

---

[26] This has been codified into the California Education Code §68130.5.

9

Bilingual Education Redux

Whereas the 1970s represented a period of growth and optimism about the obligations of school districts and states to respond to the needs of English learner (EL) students, the 1980s were spotty and mostly negative. On the legislative front, Colorado repealed its bilingual law in the late 1970s, and California let its bilingual law sunset in 1986. In the courts, the early 1980s saw several victories that translated into programs in Colorado, California, and Texas. There were several decisions, such as the ones in Idaho and Illinois, that obligated states to set standards and monitor school districts. However, the most notable case, *Castañeda v. Pickard* (1981), was somewhat of a fox dressed in the benign coat of a lamb. The case challenged the adequacy of educational programming for EL students in Raymondville Independent School District in South Texas. It was not a case in which Rice or I was counsel, though we each spoke at length to attorneys at the Texas Rural Legal Assistance. We also assisted with filing an amicus brief in the Fifth Circuit Court of Appeals.

The Fifth Circuit decision sought to add meaning to the spare language of the Equal Educational Opportunity Act of 1974, which compelled school districts to take *affirmative* steps to address the needs of ELs. On one hand, the Fifth Circuit concluded that the U.S. Congress could not have intended to impose any one educational approach on school districts in enacting the provision (20 U.S.C. §1703(F)), as the mandate was for the more general affirmative response. On the other hand, the Fifth Circuit reasoned that the U.S. Congress must not have agreed to totally leave schools to their own devices. Thus emerged a framework that courts and administrative agencies readily adopted. Simply, when an educational program was challenged, a court or agency was to determine (1) if the school district had an educational theory supported by "some" experts; (2) whether such a theory was supported by resources to carry it out; (3) whether the school district had in place a program to evaluate if the theory was working; and (4) whether, if not working, the school district was amending it in a way supported by "some" experts. The first three provisions were expressed, and the fourth was implied.

I remember discussions with Rice following this so-called victory. It was concluded that we would henceforth have limited ability to argue for any preferred program since a school district could always find some "expert" to support its educational program. We concluded that the most promising avenue of attack would concern the school districts' commitment of resources to its chosen program. Given a heightened deference to school authorities, though, a challenge would be possible but difficult. Courtroom victories after that would be few and far between. This was brought home to me by the outcome of a case we brought against Berkeley, California.

Bilingual Teachers: *Teresa P. v. Berkeley Unified School District*

Where bilingual programs were adopted as opposed to English-only and English as a second language (ESL) programs, they often were delivered by teachers with less than optimum skills. Bilingual education, in our view, called for teachers with significant training. In Berkeley Unified School District, delivery was often left to aides working under a teacher. To our experts, this seemed like a cavalier response to a crucial educational need. Berkeley argued that it had responded to each of the concerns expressed in our pleading. Our counter in *Teresa P. v. Berkeley Unified School District* (1981) was to argue that its responses were either inappropriate or too feeble.

With *Castañeda v. Pickard* (1981) as the commanding authority, these were arguments we could not win. Committed to spending whatever it took, Berkeley brought in Professor Christine Rossell from Boston University to sit at the right hand of their counsel. She had all of the enthusiasm of a born-again conservative, having once embraced desegregation and then switched sides. She was able to recruit several others to join her in providing the "expert" heft that could not be challenged by a federal judge under *Castañeda v. Pickard* (1981). In fact, we had a judge who had won his spurs prosecuting Berkeley activists in the 1960s and who moved on to the U.S. Department of Justice during President Reagan's tenure.

It is often said that one learns more in defeat than in victory. What was learned by this painful loss? First, the passivity of *Castañeda v. Pickard* (1981) seemed to be a reflection of a major swing by the courts. After putting themselves on the line during the halcyon civil rights days and finding incomplete compliance with their orders and a political backlash, many courts became less ambitious, less confident in their ability and right to force change. Second, I learned the lesson that whatever one's success has been in the past, it is crucial to constantly give a critical eye to the record you have to present and the court that will evaluate it. I am still convinced, possibly incorrectly, that if Berkeley had not been able to offer up *some* programs, we would have prevailed. However, a situation in which a school district could find some support for its response, our experts and our logic, regardless of how persuasive, had little chance of success. It is easy to be dismissive of your opponent's case, but it is crucial that you put yourself in the shoes of the judge in your case and evaluate the argument in light of where the law is—not where you wish it to be. It is better to feel the pain early and to curb your demands accordingly than to feel the pain at a time when all you can do is put a positive slant on your loss. Third, it is important that your case evaluation not be tainted by dislike or dismissal of opposing counsel. It is not unusual for a crusading young lawyer to de-monize opposing counsel—to want to crush him or her. Such sentiments infected our prosecution of this case, and they interfered with our judgment. The ideal antidote for the Berkeley loss was found 3,000 miles away in Florida.

Teacher Training: Florida Consent Decree

Even before we formed Multicultural Education, Training and Advocacy (META), Rice and I had formed a relationship with Rosa Castro Feinberg, known to all as Rosie. In the 1970s and early 1980s, Rosie had worked at a federally funded center at the University of Miami that assisted school districts with addressing equity issues. She was also active in the National Association for Bilingual Education. Her husband, who died young, had been a lawyer and icon in the early days of legal services. Possibly because of her husband's influence, Rosie had been insistent that we bring our legal skills to Florida to address what she considered an intolerable lack of programming for ELs.

In the late 1980s, Rice and Pérez took several fact-finding trips to Florida. They discovered that several nationally recognized programs in the Miami area had disguised a virtual vacuum in programming elsewhere. The most notable program, housed at Coral Way Elementary School in Coral Gables, was predictably the idiosyncratic product of the well-off, well-educated Cuban immigrants who wished to preserve their language and culture during the diaspora.

At the time, there was a perception that virtually all immi-grants were crowded into Miami-Dade County. Our research suggested that, if true at one time, it was no longer so. Recent immigrants with needs for affirmative language programs were to be found throughout the state. This was especially true in Orange County, which had seen large influxes of immigrants to work in the tourist industry serving the Walt Disney World Resort in Orlando, in central Florida counties with significant farmworker populations, and in certain larger industrial venues like Hillsborough County (home to Tampa). Even the Panhandle, in proximity to Alabama and Georgia, was affected. Outside of

Miami-Dade and Broward County, the redneck mentality that had shown hostility to African Americans reigned supreme—ready to raise its ire against any demand of immigrants. In fact, Miami-Dade and Broward badly served many of the diverse groups of Hispanics who resided there, not to mention the Haitians who claimed a significant corner of Miami.

During our deliberations about Florida, Pérez decided to move to San Francisco and join me at the West Coast META outpost. That occurrence plus Rice's aversion to Florida drew me into the case. In contrast to Berkeley, Florida presented us with a venue that had done virtually nothing in response to the needs of its immigrant population.

Our first decision was whether to bring a lawsuit against the state or against representative school districts. There were arguments to be made for each approach. The argument for a lawsuit against the state was that a victory would be statewide. The flip side was that the state's role was only to set standards and to monitor them. Florida could not be expected to actually deliver a program. Thus, enforcement against the state would be a step removed from problems faced by students.

Florida was uniquely vulnerable to litigation. Whereas most states set standards for the identification of students, mandated some range of services, and compelled teachers to have specific skills, Florida did none of these things. At best, it set aspirational goals that could not be monitored. Further, our review of practices in the state convinced us that a number of legal violations with a relationship to language infected the system statewide. The *Plyler v. Doe* (1982) mandate was often ignored, leaving undocumented students on the streets in a number of school districts. Misclassification of educationally disabled and intellectually gifted students burdened Latino and African American children. In short, there were major policy gaps that could be addressed if new policies were adequately monitored and enforced. On the other hand, suing a representative school district could get us closer to the delivery of a program and greater assurance that meaningful change would take place. We also felt that a crushing judgment against a representative school district would send a message throughout the state. In the end, we chose to sue the state. Its abdication of responsibility had been so complete that we felt we could expect major changes, which would have deep impact in school districts.

The second decision we had to make was to determine who should be the representative plaintiffs. While individuals could have represented a class of students, we believed that a broad coalition of advocacy organizations would be able to make a political statement that could hasten settlement or have weight in court. What we put together was unique for a state that had yawning divides among its ethnic groups. In the end, a Mexican American group (League of United Latin American Citizens, LULAC), a Puerto Rican organization (ASPIRA), and Cuban, Haitian, and Asian advocates joined up with the statewide National Association for the Advancement of Colored People (NAACP) to become plaintiffs. This commanded attention, and it is what we got.

On the eve of filing the lawsuit, Osvaldo Soto, the founder of a powerful Latino advocacy group in Miami and signatory to the lawsuit, received a call from Betty Castor, the Florida commissioner of education, asking to explore the possibility of settlement. When Soto approached us with Castor's proposal, we were skeptical. We had all been drawn into discussions in the past that wasted time and dissipated energy. On the other hand, we had put together a coalition that spoke louder than the lawyers. We decided that we had to hear the state out.

An initial meeting was scheduled for the state house in Tallahassee. Pérez, Rosenzweig, Rosie, and I trekked up to northern Florida for what we believed would be more of a "howdy-do" with the state leadership than a substantive session. We were ushered into an amphitheater in which we were asked to sit. Soon, the room was filled with state officials. As we began to lay out the facts that we believed would convince the state that it should roll up its sleeves and work with us to arrive at a settlement, snorts emanated from our rear. This continued throughout our presentation. When we sneaked a look at the villain, it all became apparent: a spitting image of a southern sheriff was the guilty party. After several hours of preliminary skirmishing, it was agreed to begin settlement discussions in our office in San Francisco. We had concluded that if the state was serious about making changes, they would agree to meet us on our home turf for at least some of the negotiations.

The team that landed in San Francisco was led by none other than our southern sheriff. As it turned out, his snorts must have been the product of a cold or hay fever. Lee Roberts turned out to be a blessing. Roberts was nearing the end of a long career in Florida education. He understood from his experiences how Florida had treated minorities, and he cared a lot about righting wrongs. And, we have to believe, he also saw the negotiation as an opportunity to cap his career. Of great importance, he was the chief lobbyist for the Florida Department of Education in addition to being a deputy superintendent. As we would learn, the state would need to create enabling legislation for any settlement to go into effect. We might have been education law experts, but we had no experience working with the "bubbas" in the Florida legislature on equity issues. Further, repeating a lesson learned in Denver, a person who has familiarity with the culture, history, and personnel of the system you hope to change can provide invaluable insights as you sculpt a remedial plan; Roberts was such a person.

The Florida case was primarily about linguistic access.[27] By the time we filed *League of United Latin American Citizens (LULAC) et al. v. State Board of Education* (1990), it was clear that a bilingual education mandate was not in the cards. Thus, we sought to ensure that all children had access to substantive material either through native language teaching or through other ESL-based

---

[27] While the paucity of responsive linguistic programming was the centerpiece of our effort, the lawsuit also addressed general failures of minority access to gifted and talented programs and the statewide failure to protect rights established under *Plyler v. Doe* (1982).

delivery systems. The limitations we had in prescribing our bilingual program of choice led me to believe that the whole effort would result in a pyrrhic victory unless we could ensure that the education of these children would be in the hands of *trained* and committed teachers. While a teacher training program was a component of our Denver decree, it seemed even more important in Florida, where the specific pedagogical approach was to be entrusted to teachers. The dilemma we faced was that the children in need were already in school, and we could not wait until a sufficient number of trained teachers emerged from the state's teacher education schools. Thus, we were left with devising a mandated in-service training program.

Being lawyers, we fell back on precedent. Though Florida did not mandate that teachers have an ESL or bilingual certification to teach EL students, the state did have a set of standards for obtaining such a certification. There might have been some financial reward for getting the certificate, but few teachers had one, as it was not necessary and was deemed onerous.

We were able to reach an agreement stipulating that the coursework required for the Florida certificate equated to approximately 300 hours of training. The state agreed that such a program reflected its best judgment of what was needed. Thus, we borrowed from the state's nonmandatory standard. The decree mandated that all teachers working with EL students must complete 300 hours of in-service training. As it turned out, most teachers had EL students in their classrooms, and thus most Florida teachers were compelled to complete the "META Program." The time for completion was set at several years after spending hours negotiating with the head of the United Teachers of Dade on the eve of signing the decree.

Despite pockets of grumping, most teachers completed the training. As a result of this mandate, the decree became known as the "Make Every Teacher Angry" (META) decree. Years after it was signed, we agreed to reduce this mandate in exchange for requiring all administrators to take a 70-hour course in EL theory and practice. Unless administrators, who were charged with evaluating teachers, were familiar with EL issues, our goals would not be maximized.

While in-service training is the short-term answer to addressing teacher needs, everyone agrees that education schools play a larger role in the long-term. As long as education schools have a rigorous program leading to a certificate, there is no problem. Over time, Florida determined that, given demographics of the state, all teachers needed to learn how to address EL needs. This has led some states to integrate several EL-focused courses into the general curriculum and proclaim all teachers graduating as EL certified. While it is wonderful that all teachers have some training, to declare them "qualified" watered down the previously adopted requirements. I believe this is a cutting-edge issue today in many jurisdictions.

Though teacher standards became foundational to the Florida decree, our involvement addressed virtually every aspect of service delivery—from initial identification of EL status to reclas-sification. And, it dealt with several matters that were at the periphery of programs for ELs, but cried out to be addressed. One of these matters dealt with access to gifted and talented programs. Indeed, the NAACP joined our plaintiff group on our promise to address the issue of access to these programs. We learned that gifted and talented programs had often become the province of White students through the exclusive reliance on test instruments of dubious merit. As such, access was zealously guarded. At one point, we negotiated an affirmative action avenue for African Americans and non-English speakers. In the end, we broke down reliance on IQ tests and established some mechanisms for outreach and inclusion. It was far from perfect, but a step forward.

Soon, we had reports of EL programs being segregated — placed in portables closer to the football field than the academic areas of the school. With pressure, the state addressed this. *Plyler* issues also arose. Students who lacked a Social Security card or who could not show utility bills in a parent's name (many families shared homes) were denied schooling. We also addressed these and other issues. Following the signing of the decree, we helped

Speaking at the University of South Florida about the
Florida Consent Decree, early 1990s

establish a statewide oversight organization. Stefan Rosenzweig, our local counsel who had fortuitously landed in Florida, worked assiduously with Sally Herrera, whom we hired to work with parents and other friends of the decree. Such oversight seems crucial to achieve even partial implementation of an educational reform effort of any magnitude. Though the decree was not a panacea, a 25th anniversary celebration in 2015 left one with the conclusion that much had been accomplished. As described, from the beginning, the courts have ratified the obligation of states and school districts to take meaningful steps to educate ELs while refusing to specify a methodology; *Lau v. Nichols* (1974) and *Castañeda v. Pickard* (1981) are the primary authorities. Nevertheless, states and school districts have adopted bilingual education on their own. Where properly implemented, this met their federal legal obligation.

Unz Pushback on Bilingual Education

In the mid 1990s, Ron Unz, a Silicon Valley businessman with immigrant roots, chose to use the ballot initiative process in several states to obtain voter approval for a bill to prohibit bilingual education. This did not affect the obligation to meaningfully address the need of ELs, nor did it affect federal court orders. It did not directly affect states that did not approve his initiative, nor the many that did not have bilingual programs. But, his success in California, Massachusetts, and Arizona put a damper on a major educational initiative led by Latinos over the preceding three decades.

The ballot initiative process is perceived by some to be an egalitarian way around legislatures dominated by the rich and powerful. In California during the 1990s, two ballot initiatives—Proposition 187 (1994) and Proposition 227 (1998)—provided evidence that this mechanism is a useful tool of the wealthy to counter the emerging power of minorities in some legislatures and to tap into majority discontent with perceived minority advances.

At the time, bilingual education was viewed by many Whites and some African Americans as a program designed specifically to benefit Latinos exclusively while being paid for with limited tax dollars. Unfortunately, arguments about teaching children in a language they could understand were often unheard. Instead, many saw it as a way of asserting Latino power. The fact that the value of native language instruction was oversold by proponents while being undercut by inadequate implementation in many school districts did not help the case.

In court to enjoin Proposition 187 with Robert Rubin, Lawyer's Committee; Ralph Abascal, California Rural Legal Assistance; and Marta Jimenez, MALDEF. Photo by Maya Alleruzzo; used with permission of the *Recorder*/ALM Media Properties.

Unz got the signatures to put an anti–bilingual education initiative on the California ballot, Proposition 227 (1998). He successfully tapped into Anglo malaise in the general election and was wise enough to ratify the federal mandate for affirmative programming, while tamping down on bilingual education. This undercut the legal challenge that META, the Mexican American Legal Defense Fund (MALDEF), and others mounted. Unz was similarly successful in Massachusetts (General Law 71.A), where Rice participated in a political fight but chose not to engage in a fruitless legal challenge. Although the Unz effort was beaten back in Colorado, where our federal court order would have trumped state law, it did little to revive the bilingual movement.

In 2016, when bilingual instruction had dwindled to almost nothing, another ballot measure, Proposition 58 (2016), reinstated much of what was quashed by Unz in California. It remains to be seen whether the removal of Unz's restrictions will result in a major push for bilingual instruction in the state. It is my belief that to enable broad-scale bilingual education, a number of strategic errors should be addressed. First, bilingual programs should be built up, not dropped on school districts as mandates. A major problem with our earlier approach was that it relied on the argument that native language was required for equal access. This led to mandates being imposed before the infrastructure to deliver quality programs was available. Mandating native instruction without having teachers capable of delivery is setting yourself up for failure. Of course, we were not oblivious to this problem, but instead we chose to believe that you would never get the teachers and materials without first creating the demand by mandating programs. While this argument resonates, it carries with it a terrible cost and provides the seeds for a backlash. Second, no educational program should be sold as a magic bullet—something that many proponents did with bilingual instruction. Much more is needed to address the issues that affect low-income children of color. It is tempting to overpromise, but it is a bad idea.

10

Continued Legal Battles

A Swipe at Immigrants Through the Ballot Box: Proposition 187

Another California initiative, Proposition 187 (1994), would have stripped undocumented individuals of virtually all rights, including those won in *Plyler v. Doe* (1982) and *Leticia A. v. Board of Regents* (1985). Backed by California Governor Pete Wilson, the state initiative was approved by voters. Challenges were mounted in both federal and state courts, and educational gains were fully preserved through victories in both courts (*LULAC v. Wilson*, 1997; *Pedro A. v. Dawson*, 1994; *Jesus Doe, et al. v. Regents of the University of California, et al.*, 1997).[28] The entire initiative was ultimately enjoined in federal court. The injunctions were based on the fact that the federal government had already addressed many of the issues and had restricted many of the alien rights at issue. *Plyler v. Doe* (1982) was cited as a constitutional prohibition against the denial of schooling to undocumented children.

Separate and Unequal: Addressing the Inequality of Resources

Possibly the most ambitious case that I was involved with targeted the Los Angeles Unified School District. The case,

---

[28] Note that the state cases challenging the *Plyler* violation in elementary and secondary education, *Pedro A. v. Dawson* (1994) and *Jesus Doe, et al. v. Regents of the University of California, et al.* (1997), were limited to education violations and each resolved in favor of the plaintiffs.

Rodríguez v. Los Angeles Unified School District (LAUSD) (1992), while having a significant outcome, never really lived up to the ambitions we had going in. In the late 1980s, I was approached by Carol Smith, who had been appointed to direct educational litigation at the Legal Aid Foundation of Los Angeles. Smith had spent years as a fierce advocate for the disadvantaged in Los Angeles, though she was relatively new to education.

Our initial discussions revolved around the issue of over-crowding in the Chicano schools in inner-city Los Angeles. As a result of its inability to build schools to meet demand in these areas, the school district had chosen to unilaterally bus some students to the far reaches of the San Fernando Valley and to place those who remained in their neighborhoods in year-round schools. Despite arguments from the school district that year-round schools and one-way busing promoted academic excellence, most parents and students in the affected schools saw this as blatant discrimination. As we explored the ramifications of this issue, our interest was tweaked by related information. We found out that schools in the inner city were disproportionately staffed by teachers with emergency credentials and limited experience. It seemed to us that the kids with the greatest needs were being taught by those least able. Given the unattractiveness of the schools and the lack of skilled teachers, the dropout problem became understandable.

We recruited the American Civil Liberties Union, the Mexican American Legal Defense Fund (MALDEF), the Western Center on Law and Poverty, and San Fernando Valley Legal Services to join us in a broad-based challenge to what we perceived as discrimination in the allocation of two chief resources: school houses and teachers. As we studied this issue, we concluded that placing students in oversized schools with inexperienced teachers produced another powerful claim. Teachers' salaries make up the lion's share of a school's cost because salaries are highly related to experience and certification. Furthermore, overcrowding results in economies of scale. Thus, we reasoned that the per-pupil cost of educating low-income, minority students must be less than the cost of educating students in more affluent parts of town. School finance litigation in the state via *Serrano v. Priest* (1971) suggested that this would constitute a violation of the California Constitution.

As the case evolved and greater amounts of data and information became available, we began to tweak our demands. After speaking to Professor Linda Darling-Hammond and other experts at Teachers College, Columbia University, we concluded that we needed to reframe our complaint. Early on, we had concluded that we had no interest in forcing older teachers to work in inner-city schools; it seemed to be educationally counterproductive and fruitless. Second, we determined that averaging experience did not tell a very compelling story. Rather, as we looked at the data, it suggested that inner-city schools were polarized. They usually contained a few older teachers, who were often unwanted elsewhere, and large numbers of undercredentialed teachers. While young, enthusiastic teachers were a good thing in moderation, large numbers of inexperienced teachers working without guidance was not a desirable outcome. We also learned that there was opposition from inner-city residents to build additional schools. In crowded inner-city areas, the building of new schools inevitably led to the displacement of residents who had limited housing choices.

After several years of intense pretrial litigation, the school district suggested that we explore the possibility of settlement. In addition to the belief that a settlement was more likely to result in change than an imposed remedy, another factor nagged at us: Our case was primarily based on establishing a racial nexus to the disparities we had uncovered. While it was possible to create a graph that roughly reflected a racial division of negative impacts in schools with the highest percentages of Black and Latino students, the schools we had to characterize as predominantly Anglo were only Anglo in relation to the most impacted Black and Latino schools. White flight had led to schools in which Anglos were still in the minority. This effect had been exacerbated in Los

Angeles by the busing program to relieve overcrowding. This fact raised concerns about going to trial.

Thus, several years of negotiations ensued. The final agreement wove together the claim about underqualified teachers with that of financial disparities. Even before it actually went into effect, it was modified dramatically. The original settlement was grounded on two points. First, financial disparities between schools were deemed to constitute discrimination. It should be noted that the discrimination was the mirror opposite of that usually alleged in school finance lawsuits. In those cases, lesser money is available to lower-income school districts who must buy lesser educational commodities. In our case, lesser commodities were allocated to low-income students of color, thus resulting in financial disparity. The second point was a school district imperative, especially during a period of declining revenues. The school district insisted that the remedy be financially neutral. This led to a settlement that relied upon shifting dollars from schools with above-average revenues to those with revenues below the average. Although this seemed to meet our respective needs, it turned out that the school district quickly determined that it was no Robin Hood. The hue and cry of taking money from schools that already felt like they had too little was not politically palatable. By the time the first disbursements occurred, the school district had managed to squeeze some other part of its budget to meet the terms of the agreement. It is my recollection that approximately $15 to $20 million was allocated to low-spending schools each year that the agreement was in place, roughly 10 years. But, our goal had not been to merely reallocate funds to low-spending schools. We had set out to get better prepared teachers before these students. Thus, the next element of the decree.

Each school that received money under the decree was to use that money to enhance the skills of beginning teachers or to provide them with resources to mitigate the consequences of their inexperience. At the time of the settlement, school-based budgeting was perceived to be a powerful tool to stimulate school sites to take needed responsibility for the children in their schools. We bought into the argument that having financial decisions made centrally was a powerful cause for school failure. While giving money directly to the schools led to creative programming in many schools, evidence trickled up that many schools were using the money as general funds—notwithstanding trainings and guidelines implementing the decree. As time went on, we increased the reporting requirements and the obligations on the central administration to monitor the funds. It is hard to say how much this curtailed the natural force of the schools to broadly use the money to plug holes rather than address the issues for which the money had been allocated. In any event, anyone besotted by school-based budgeting ought to understand this very real danger and assure adequate monitoring and enforcement so that monies designated for certain needs in fact reach their targets.

Even though the final agreement made clear that no teacher was to be involuntarily transferred under the agreement, the teacher's union (United Teachers Los Angeles) chose to challenge it. They were able to convince the unions representing district administrators and paraprofessionals to join them. A settlement of this sort had to be approved by the Court. After several weeks of hearings in which the school district joined us in battling the unions, the Court approved the settlement in its entirety.

Clearly, much good came from the settlement. Going in, we believed that we could turn around the Los Angeles Unified School District and influence matters nationally; this was a wildly optimistic stance. Nationally, stories about teacher disparities almost certainly laid the groundwork for federal legislation, which began to address the issue. Still today, the problem of getting trained, experienced, and concerned teachers into inner-city schools persists. Maybe it is time for another run at the problem.

Approximately 7 or 8 years after our case was dismissed, a conservative effort was initiated using the teacher disparity issue to challenge teacher tenure laws in California. They argued that by allowing teachers to choose assignments based on seniority and by making it prohibitive to fire a tenured teacher, these laws resulted in the problem we tackled in *Rodríguez v. Los Angeles Unified School District (LAUSD)* (1992). While there is no doubt some truth to this charge, it is simplistic. Clearly, incentives, and not merely financial incentives, need be put into place to attract and retain good people to difficult, but potentially rewarding, assignments. Abolition of tenure laws has the potential to dissuade many young individuals from going into the teaching profession, a profession seen as tenuous at best. Though I question the broad attack on tenure, civil rights advocates, often steeped in lore about the victories of unions in battling employer over-reaching, must not hesitate to take on unions when appropriate. Clearly, aspects of union contracts are often self-serving to the involved parties and dismissive of those who are not at the table—the students.

A Final Defense of Postsecondary Access for Undocumented Students

Given the cyclical nature of educational reform and the inevitable pushback against victories that benefit minorities, it is not surprising that the battle that concluded my career was one to preserve the gains started by the *Leticia A. v. Board of Regents* (1985) litigation, which made tuition costs for undocumented students the same as those of state residents in California.

Soon after the millennium, anti-immigrant forces targeted state legislation that granted in-state tuition to undocumented immigrants. Federal legislation, which we had considered in drafting AB 540 (the bill that put into gear the ruling from *Leticia A. v. Board of Regents*, 1985), was seen as violated by these kinds of laws.[29] Kris Kobach, law professor and hero to the anti-immigrant

---

[29] 8 U.S.C.§1621 barred public benefits to an undocumented student *unless* a state law "affirmatively" provided for such eligibility. To satisfy these demands, we drafted AB 540 to specify eligibility for undocumented students meeting 8 U.S. Code §1621 requirements. We also spelled out that in-state tuition was being granted on conditions other than residency, such as attendance for an extended time in California public schools; other states followed suit.

movement, led the charge. His first venue was his home state of Kansas. Kobach sued on behalf of citizens he claimed had to pay more as a result of the state's generosity. We intervened on behalf of several Latino organizations after the Kansas attorney general, an ideological colleague of Kobach, refused to defend the statute. The Kansas law was upheld by the lower federal courts and review was sought in the U.S. Supreme Court (*Day v. Bond*, 2007).

By the time Kobach sought U.S. Supreme Court review, I was retired and temporarily living in Mexico. I wrote the opposition to certiorari in Mexico, sending handwritten drafts for typing and filing to Gene Baloun, my co-counsel, who was with a Kansas City law firm. We often laughed at how exposure of this venue for writing would confirm for Kobach and his allies that the whole effort was a Mexican conspiracy. In any event, we were successful in convincing the Court not to grant the review (*Day v. Bond*, 2007). Kobach filed a similar suit in California, which went to the California Supreme Court. Again, the undocumented students prevailed (*Martínez v. Regents of the University of California*, 2010).

A final anecdote from the Kansas case: Despite her undocumented status, one of the young individuals we represented had testified before the Kansas legislature in favor of the bill, which would enable her and others to attend college. Her story was captured in the local media. Like so many of those who benefited from these bills, she had come to the United States as a minor and had succeeded in school well beyond the usual expectations for a child of poverty. Her testimony pointed to a career of service to the community in which she lived, and that story captured the imagination of an anonymous admirer. When I drove out to Manhattan, the home of Kansas State University, to discuss her participation in the lawsuit, I was enlisted to carry a suitcase full of new clothes. By all accounts, her wardrobe (but not her intellect) would have been a barrier to successful integration into the Kansas State University community. Suspecting as much, the anonymous admirer had chosen to assist her in any way possible. He had sent a message to the nonprofit which had joined with her in securing passage of the law. The clothes came with the message that he had assisted with the college education of several of his grandchildren, but he now wanted to make sure that a person who really deserved to succeed did so. It is my sense that if America was as generous as this unknown gentleman, this country would be a much better place.

11

Conclusion

Approaching the age of 80, my wife Emma has found a new vocation. Rather than teaching (something she did with great success in Chihuahua, Cambridge, and Oakland), and rather than encouraging student success through support (many former Oakland Unified School District students point to the Latino Honor Roll as transformative), she has become a hard-bitten advocate. Our pillow talk now frequently addresses such questions as how to pressure schools to hire more bilingual teachers or how to ensure equitable funding for Latino students.

Not infrequently, when Emma tries to draw ideas from me, I pull the pillow over my head. This, despite—or possibly because of—having spent a lifetime of advocacy on the very subjects in which she is engaged. I see my reaction as akin to that of the federal judges who took on complex reform cases in the 1960s and 1970s only to find that even the majesty of the law and the imperiousness of the judiciary could only affect partial change. A number of these former activist-judges seemed to find subtle reasons to rule against needy civil rights plaintiffs. After a lifetime of national advocacy on many of the issues that engage Emma locally, I, too, am inclined to throw up my hands. Certainly, our litigation has not been a silver bullet. So many low-income students of color still seem to be impossibly far from a life of economic security.

I fear that my despair infuses a broader polity and saps energy away from a need to keep inching closer to the goal of cracking the spiral of educational failure. Indeed, this despair has the potential to threaten public education or to justify expanding inequitable allocations in the belief that one should not throw good money after bad.

But I know Emma is right to keep on trucking. Improvements, not panaceas, are possible and important. I am confident that the fights described here, and the fights of so many others, have changed the complexion of America. Just looking at my personal ledger, a small microcosm of the whole, there is cause for optimism—optimism that advocacy, which includes political pressure, grassroots involvement, and litigation, can work, if imperfectly. Hundreds of thousands of undocumented kids have gone to school and certainly emerged to a better life. If we had stayed home and not brought *Plyler v. Doe* (1982) and *Leticia A. v. Board of Regents* (1985) forward or if we had not cleaned up the detritus with state acts based on AB 540, this would not have been the case. Indeed, one can trace the concepts and detail of Deferred Action for Childhood Arrivals back to the triggers for AB 540 that Robert Rubin and I developed in our offices. And, those efforts built on arguments we advanced and the court found persuasive in *Plyler v. Doe* (1982). Stay home? Forget it!

Before we took on teacher inequalities in *Rodríguez v. Los Angeles Unified School District (LAUSD)* (1992), they were discussed only in intellectual circles. While our remedy fell short in Los Angeles, the issue is now out of the closet. Recent iterations of federal education law have contained responses to the problem. California requires the collection of teacher data, which is awaiting the next generation of advocates. Again, local advocacy led by the litigation has moved a conversation that I believe cannot be stopped.

It is certainly possible to look at bilingual education and desegregation efforts as a glass half-full—or worse. But I think it is fairer to say that they have yielded less than promised, while freeing up many to improve their lot. In the early 1970s, the U.S. Commission on Civil Rights documented the widespread punishment of students for speaking Spanish in school. At the same time, one needed a microscope to find a Chicano lawyer or doctor. The bilingual education movement, by demanding that schools celebrate students' culture, played a role in changing the equation—far from perfectly, but substantially.

Similarly, so long as *de jure* segregation continued, few Black or Chicano children would have had the confidence to function competitively in broader society. Having just come from a celebration exhorting college-going Latinas to "love themselves," I realized that marginalized groups still carry a weight that those who come from the dominant culture carry less often, but these young women were acknowledging their accomplishments from the perch of a college campus—an unlikely venue if they still labored under the weight of *de jure* segregation. Yes, *de facto* segregation and White privilege require an agenda, but it is an agenda that can be fought.

In sum, one need not be a Pollyanna to follow in the footsteps of Emma and all the other advocates who keep the fires burning. Meaningful battles will always be there to be fought. Some of those battles will be to pin down victories mentioned herein, or to build upon them—that is okay. After all, none were panaceas.

References

Acosta, O. (1972). *The autobiography of a brown buffalo.* San Francisco, CA: Straight Arrow Press.

Alvarado v. El Paso Independent School District, 426 F. Supp. 575 (W.D. Tex. 1976).

Alvarado v. El Paso Independent School District, 593 F. Supp. 577 (5th Cir. 1979).

Amos v. Board of School Directors of City of Milwaukee, 408 F. Supp. 765 (E.D. Wis. 1976).

Bakke v. Regents of the University of California, 18 Cal. 3d 34 (Cal. 1976).

Bennett, M., & Reynoso, C. (1972). California Rural Legal Assistance (CRLA): Survival of a poverty law practice. *Chicano Law Review, 1*(1), 1-79.

Black Voters v. McDonough, 421 F. Supp. 165 (D. Mass. 1976).

Blair v. Pitchess, 5 Cal. 3d 258 (Cal. 1971).

Brown v. Board of Education of Topeka, 347 U.S. 483 (1954).

California Governor's Commission on the Los Angeles Riots. (1965). *Violence in the city: An end or a beginning? A report.* Los Angeles, CA: Author.

Castañeda v. Pickard, 648 F. 2d. 989 (5th Cir. 1981).

Castro v. State of California, 2 Cal. 3d. 223 (Cal. 1970).

Certain Named and Unnamed Non-Citizen Children v. Texas, 49 U.S.L.W. 3133, 3134 (5th Cir. 1980).

Crawford v. Los Angeles Board of Education, 458 U.S. 527 (1982).

Columbus Board of Education v. Penick, 443 U.S. 449 (1979).

Comité de Padres de Familia v. Riles, 13 C.L.R. 390 (Cal. Super. 1979).

Cotton, S. E. (1984). Alaska's 'Molly Hootch case': High schools and the Village Voice. *Educational Research Quarterly, 8*(4), 30-43.

Davis v. School District of City of Pontiac, Inc., 309 F. Supp. 734 (E.D. Mich. 1970).

Day v. Bond, 511 F. 3d 1030 (10th Cir. 2007).

Dayton Board of Education v. Brinkman, 443 U.S. 526 (1979).

Doe v. Plyler, 458 F. Supp. 569 (E.D. Tex. 1978).

Fisher v. University of Texas, 570 U.S. __ (2013).

Friendly, F. W. (Director/Producer), Lowe, D. (Producer), & Murrow, E. R. (Producer). (1960). *Harvest of shame* [DVD]. New York, NY: Docurama.

Goss v. López, 419 U.S. 565 (1975).

Grutter v. Bollinger, 539 U.S. 306 (2003).

Hernandez v. Houston Independent School District, 558 S.W. 2d. 121 (Tex. Civ. App. 1977).

Hernandez v. Texas, 374 U.S. 475 (1954).

Hootch v. Alaska State-Operated School System, 536 P. 2d 793 (Alaska 1975).

Hubbard, R. W. (1973). Up against the wall redneck mother [Recorded by Jerry Jeff Walker]. On Viva Terlingua [MP3 file]. Nashville, TN: MCA Nashville Records.

Idaho Migrant Council v. Board of Education, 647 F. 2d. 69 (9th Cir. 1981).

In Re Alien Children Ed. Litigation, 501 F. Supp. 544 (S.D. Tex. 1980).

Jesus Doe v. Regents of the University of California, No. 965-090 (Superior Court of the State of California in and for the City of San Francisco 1994).

Johnson, L. B. (1965). Commencement address at Howard University: To fulfill these rights. In *Public Papers of the President of the United States, Lyndon B. Johnson, 1965* (Vol. 2). Washington, DC: Government Printing Office.

Keyes v. School District No. 1, 303 F. Supp. 279 (D.Colo. 1969).

Keyes v. School District No. 1, 413 U.S. 189 (1973).

Keyes v. School District No. 1, 521 F. 2d 465 (10th Cir. 1975).

Keyes v. School District No. 1, 576 F. Supp. 1503, 1516 (D.Colo. 1983).

Lau v. Nichols, 414 U.S. 563 (1974).

Leticia A., et al. v. Board of Regents of the University of California, No. 588-982-4 (Superior Court of the State of California in and for the County of Alameda, 1985).

Lopez v. Williams, 372 F. Supp. 1279 (S.D. Ohio 1974).

League of United Latin American Citizens (LULAC) et al. v. State Board of Education, No. 90-1913 (S.D. Fl. 1990).

League of United Latin American Citizens (LULAC) v. Wilson, 997 F. Supp. 1244 (C.D. Cal. 1997).

Martínez v. Regents of the University of California, 117 Cal. Rptr. 3d 359 (Cal. 2010).

Mendez v. Westminister School District, 64 F. Supp. 544 (S.D. Cal. 1946).

Milliken v. Bradley, 418 U.S. 717 (1974).

Morales v. Shannon, 516 F. 2d 411, 413 (5th Cir.), cert. denied, 423 U.S. 1034 (1975).

Morgan v. Hennigan, 379 F. Supp. 410 (D.Mass. 1974).

Morris v. Williams, 67 Cal. 2d. 733 (Cal. 1967).

Nellis, A. (2016). *The color of justice: Racial and ethnic disparity in state prisons.* Washington, DC: The Sentencing Project.

Pedro A. v. Dawson, No. 965089 (Superior Court of the State of California in and for the City of San Francisco 1994).

Perera, J. H. (2014). Controversies re-emerge in fight over Texas textbooks. *Texas Chronicle.* Retrieved from https://www.chron.com/news/houston-texas/article/Controversies-key-issues-in-fight-over-Texas-5778982.php

Plyler v. Doe, 628 F. 2d 448 (5th Cir. 1980).

Plyler v. Doe, 457 U.S. 202 (1982).

Rakove, M. L. (1976). *Don't make no waves . . . don't back no losers: An insider's analysis of the Daley machine.* Bloomington, IN: Indiana University Press.

Regents of the University of California v. Bakke, 438 U.S. 265 (1978).

Rhode Island Society for Autistic Children (RISAC) v. Board of Regents, Civ. Action No. 5081 (D.R.I. 1975).

Rodríguez v. Los Angeles Unified School District (LAUSD), No. C611358 (Cal. Super. 1992).

Romero v. Weakley, 131 F. Supp. 818 (S.D. Cal. 1955).

Ross v. Houston Independent School District, 457 F. Supp. 18 (S.D. Tex. 1977).

Roos, P. (1984). *Social scientists, lawyers, and community working for educational reform.* London, UK: University of London Institute for Education.

San Antonio Independent School District v. Rodríguez, 411 U.S. 1 (1973).

Serrano v. Priest, 487 P. 2d 1241 (Cal. 1971).

Sniadach v. Family Finance Corp, 395 U.S. 337 (1969).

Superior Court of the State of California, County of San Diego, Petition for Writ of Mandate No. 66625 (1931).

Soria v. Oxnard School District Board of Trustees, 328 F. Supp. 155 (C.D. Cal. 1971).

Soria v. Oxnard School District Board of Trustees, 467 F. 2d 59 (9th Cir. 1972).

Teresa P. v. Berkeley Unified School District, 724 F. Supp. 698 (N.D. Cal. 1989).

United States Commission on Civil Rights. (1971). *Ethnic isolation of Mexican-Americans in the public schools of the Southwest.* Washington, DC: Government Printing Office.

United States of America v. Texas Education Agency et al., 579 F. 2d 910 (5th Cir. 1978).

United States of America v. State of Texas, 342 F. Supp. 24 (E.D. Tex. 1971).

United States of America v. State of Texas, 506 F. Supp. 405 (E.D. Tex. 1981).

Wagner, C. (2017, January). *Segregation then and now: How to move toward a more perfect union.* Alexandria, VA: Center for Public Education. Retrieved from https://www.nsba.org/-/media/NSBA/File/cpe-school-segregation-then-and-now-report-january-2017.pdf

Appendix: Definitions and Acronyms

Key Terms

Law Students Civil Rights Research Council (LSCRRC): A multiracial, student-run organization in the United States founded in 1963 to support the southern civil rights movement.

Legal Services Corporation (LSC): An independent 501(c)(3) non-profit corporation established by the U.S. Congress in 1974 to provide legal aid for low-income Americans with the mission of promoting equal access to justice.

Office of Economic Opportunity (OEO): A federal agency created by President Lyndon B. Johnson via the Economic Opportunity Act of 1964. The agency was tasked with distributing funding for vocational training and overseeing programs such as Job Corps, Community Action Program, Head Start, and Volunteers in Service to America (VISTA). The OEO was abolished in 1981 with responsibilities distributed to other federal agencies.

Western Center on Law and Poverty (WCLP): A California-based legal services support center focused on housing, health care, and racial justice for low-income residents of the state.

Legal and Educational Acronyms

ACBE: American Coalition for Bilingual Education
ACLU: American Civil Liberties Union
CDF: Children's Defense Fund
CLE: Center for Law and Education
DACA: Deferred Action for Childhood Arrivals
DL: Dual language
ED: Department of Education
EEOA: Equal Educational Opportunity Act
EL: English learners
ELL: English language learners
ESEA: Elementary and Secondary Education Act
ESL: English as a second language
ESSA: Every Student Succeeds Act
LEP: Limited English proficient
LSC: Legal Services Corporation
LULAC: League of United Latin American Citizens
MALDEF: Mexican American Legal Defense Fund
META: Multicultural Education, Training and Advocacy
NAACP LDF: National Association for the Advancement of Colored People Legal Defense and Education Fund
NABE: National Association for Bilingual Education
OCR: Office for Civil Rights
OEO: Office of Economic Opportunity
SNLS: Southeast Neighborhood Legal Services
TBE: Transitional bilingual education
USCCR: U.S. Commission on Civil Rights
WCLP: Western Center on Law and Poverty

Center for Applied Linguistics

The mission of the Center for Applied Linguistics (CAL) is to promote language learning and cultural understanding by serving as a trusted source for research, resources, and policy analysis. Through its work, CAL seeks solutions to issues involving language and culture as they relate to access and equity in education and society around the globe.

CAL also has a set of core values that guide all of our endeavors and help us focus our efforts more effectively. These values are outlined below and reflect CAL's strong commitment to promoting access, equity, and mutual understanding for linguistically and culturally diverse people around the world.

- Languages and cultures are important individual and societal resources.
- All languages, dialects, and cultures deserve to be respected and cultivated.
- Multilingualism is beneficial for individuals and society.
- Effective language education should be widely available.
- Accurate information should be the basis for policies and practices that involve language and culture.
- Language skills and cultural knowledge should be valued in work situations.
- Language and cultural differences should not be obstacles to personal or group success or well-being.

4646 40th Street, NW
Washington, DC 20016-1859
Phone: 202-362-0700

Website: www.cal.org